ADVENT/CHRISTMAS

**INTERPRETING
THE LESSONS OF
THE CHURCH YEAR**

**WILLIAM
H. WILLIMON**

**PROCLAMATION 5
SERIES B**

FORTRESS PRESS   MINNEAPOLIS

To Stanley M. Hauerwas, Friend

PROCLAMATION 5
Interpreting the Lessons of the Church Year
Series B, Advent/Christmas

Scripture quotations, unless translated by the author or otherwise noted, are from the New Revised Standard Version Bible, copyright © 1989 by the Division of Christian Education of the National Council of Churches of Christ in the U.S.A. and used by permission.

Cover and interior design: Spangler Design Team

Library of Congress Cataloging-in-Publication Data
(Revised for Ser. B, v. 1-4)

Proclamation 5.

   Contents: ser. A. [2] Epiphany / Pheme Perkins —
[etc.] — ser. B. [1] Advent/Christmas / William H.
Willimon — [2] Epiphany / David Rhoads — [3] Lent /
Thomas Hoyt, Jr. — [4] Holy Week / Walter Wink.
   1. Bible—Homiletical use.   2. Bible—Liturgical
lessons, English.   I. Perkins, Pheme.
BS534.5.P765   1993   251   92-22973
ISBN 0-8006-4185-X (ser. B, Advent/Christmas)
ISBN 0-8006-4186-8 (ser. B, Epiphany)
ISBN 0-8006-4187-6 (ser. B, Lent)
ISBN 0-8006-4188-4 (ser. B, Holy Week)

The paper used in this publication meets the minimum requirements of American National Standard for Information Sciences—Permanence of Paper for Printed Library Materials, ANSI Z329.48-1984. ∞™

Manufactured in the U.S.A.   AF 1-4185

97   96   95   94   93   1   2   3   4   5   6   7   8   9   10

CONTENTS

Introduction

ADVENT AS REVOLUTION

I noted, after my first Advent/Christmas at our university chapel, that sermons during this season are among the year's most controversial. Why? After all, we are only "getting ready for Christmas." Why should such yuletide preparation provoke resistance in the ears of a university congregation? Is not Christmas among the year's most joyous seasons?

One person emerged after an Advent service at another university chapel and accused me of "promoting irresponsible passivity" in the sermon. "You should remind us that 'We are educated, responsible people who have been given the gifts to make the world a better place,'" he said. He heard the sermon as an excuse for political quietism—do nothing because God comes in Jesus to do it for (or to) us.

Yet what is the preacher to say, stuck with the repeated Advent Gospel assertion that God really has come in Jesus Christ to do for us what we could *not* do for ourselves? How can the preacher calibrate the Hebrew Scriptures' prophetic announcement that history had again become interesting not because we had at last gotten organized but because God was moving among us? Who could blame the Advent preacher's sermon on the assigned Epistle for sounding as if we were at the end of something, call it death or birth? In short, my critic had gotten more than a whiff of eschatology and found its odor distinctly offensive to his activist-educated, progressive sensibilities. He, like most of us, would rather get better than be born again. He, like most of us, wants a world improved rather than made new.

Note that nearly all Advent lections are eschatological in focus. This is the season of "the last (Greek: *eschatos*) things," the beginning of winter death in nature, the ending of another year. Yet it is also the beginning of the church year, a time of birth at Bethlehem, a time when we know not whether to name what is happening among us as "ending" or "beginning" for it feels both as if something old is dying and something new is being born.

Christian eschatology, like Jewish eschatology before it, makes a claim about the future in which the creator of the world at the beginning is fully revealed as the world's redeemer at the end. Eschatology is more a matter of Who? than When? "The end" is not so much a matter of chronology (When?) but rather a debate over who, in the end, is in charge. Or, as H. Richard Niebuhr put it, eschatology "does not lie in the time-factor so much as on the God-factor" (*The Responsible Self: An Essay in Christian*

Moral Philosophy [New York: Harper & Row, 1978], 167). The hope for the coming of Christ in fullness (Christ's parousia) has nothing to do with the hope engendered by wishful thinking, a positive mental attitude, or creative social programming. Our hope is grounded in the promise of God and in our weekly celebration and reiteration of that promise in our Sunday worship.

Advent texts promise us that, when all has been said and done by God, in us as individuals, in our political/social/economic structures, in the whole cosmos, God will reign. In the Western church, as the church made peace with the present order after the fourth century, the pushy political, extravagantly cosmic claims of Christian eschatology shrunk to more modest, individualized, *ars moriendi* pastoral care concerns for individual souls being prepared for another life beyond death.

Perhaps the most important contribution of twentieth-century biblical studies (see E. P. Sanders, *Jesus and Judaism* [Philadelphia: Fortress, 1985]) has been the rediscovery that our Scripture is inescapably, irreducibly eschatological (even though most of historical criticism had no ecclesial way to take the Bible's eschatology with political seriousness). Older preaching as the preparation of individual souls for individual salvation from individual sin and death, and newer preaching as the infusion of self-esteem into depressed individuals, will not do justice to these Advent/Christmas texts. What God is doing among us, for us, often despite us, is large, cosmic, political, nothing less than "a new heaven and a new earth" (Rev. 21:1).

Our individual hope is grounded in the promised cosmic dismantling and reconstructive transformation which God is doing in the whole world. John Howard Yoder was pointing to the eschatological nature of our hope when he suggested that the word "revolution" was a bit closer to the root meaning of *euangelion* than merely "good news" (John Howard Yoder, *The Original Revolution: Essays on Christian Pacifism* [Scottdale, PA: Herald Press, 1972]). The good news of Advent is that we are being met, reconstructed by a revolutionary God who intends to make all things new.

And therein lies the rub. We enjoy telling ourselves that our uneasiness with these texts—God as the thief in the night, the cosmic upheaval, the weird birth—has to do with our modern, scientific sophistication. We can believe that the world might melt down in our nuclear self-destruction or ecological disaster but not that God might end what God began in an act of divine judgment. We've got the whole world in our hands. The U.N. urges us to "Save the Planet." With Carol Christ we sing, "I found God in myself and I loved her fiercely" (*Womanspirit Rising* [New York: Harper & Row, 1979], 277), "liberation" as the triumph of the autonomous ego of the liberal West.

We enjoy believing that the world's future is exclusively up to us and feel either guilty or empowered by that belief, depending upon the particular nature of the self-deception at work in us. We think of church as a place to come to get energized to live up to our Promethean responsibilities to care for the world and do not enjoy being told that God may have a very different world in mind than the one we presume to preserve through our earnest activism.

More than likely, Advent eschatology offends us for more mundane reasons. I am at church seeking personal advice for how to have a happy marriage or how to get along with the boss next week, only to have Advent wrench my gaze off my subjectivity in its insistence that whatever God is about in the advent of Jesus, it is something quite large, quite cosmic, quite strange and humanly unmanageable, something more significant than me. I am not the master of history.

So let us begin with the honest admission. Our real problem with these Advent/Christmas texts is largely political rather than merely intellectual. A great deal will depend on our social location. If you tell me, living in Durham with two healthy, well-fed, well-futured children, "This world is ending. God has little vested interest in the present order," I shall hear it as bad news.

However, for a mother in a barrio in Mexico City who has lost four of her six children to starvation to hear, "This present world is not what God had in mind. God is not finished, indeed is now moving, to break down and to rebuild in Jesus," I presume that would sound something like gospel. For her, the texts you will be asked to deliver this Advent/Christmas are not (as has been charged by some liberal critics) an invitation to "pie-in-the-sky, by-and-by" theology. They are a series of Molatov cocktails meant to ignite a revolutionary conflagration. They begin in the ghettos, as whispered expectation among pushy slaves, as the clench-fisted yearning of displaced Hebrew refugees, as the cry of a baby born in a backstreet to an occupied people.

A great deal depends, in regard to our receptivity to these texts, on where we happen to be standing at the time when we get the news, "God is coming."

Eschatology, as John Howard Yoder says, is the peculiar way we Christians remind ourselves of the weird truth that "There is no significance to human effort and, strictly speaking, no history unless life can be seen in terms of ultimate goals. The *eschaton*, the 'Last Thing,' the End-Event, imparts to life a meaningfulness which it would not otherwise have. This is what we mean by eschatology: a hope which, defying present frustration, defines a present position in terms of the yet unseen goals which give it meaning" (*The Original Revolution*, 56).

CHRISTMAS AS CRISIS

"The real meaning of Christmas" is that the future is God's and our fate has been made God's own. In this realization is our hope—our last, best hope. In this hope we wait, having been graciously given time. In this waiting time between Christ's first advent and the next, we need not wait in wallowing self-despair. Our wait is a time of activity for us actively to tell and to show the adventure of living in a world and in a time when God is among us. By these texts, we are freed from the vain, exhausting attempt to make history come out right on our terms, to assume that our lives have no significance other than that meaning that we make for ourselves. We can breathe.

Older historical criticism of Scripture made much of the observation that some of these texts were written by early Christians who expected the immanent, apocalyptic end of the world, an end that did not come about during their generation.

Quite to the contrary, Christians assert that we have indeed seen the end. For us, the world came to an end, not on Christmas but on Good Friday, when the world did its absolute worst in the death of Jesus. There was fought the decisive Armageddon between God and the powers. That battle was in the end resolved in favor of God's lordship over our existence. We therefore look at the Advent of Jesus from this eschatological perspective, from the knowledge that God's kingdom has been established, to the end that the kingdoms of this world have been thrown into permanent and (alas, for those kingdoms) fatal crisis.

The world in which we exist will not go on indefinitely—indeed, need not go on indefinitely—since, in the deepest sense, this world has ended in the life, death, and resurrection of Jesus. Admittedly, our recognition of that requires great imagination on our part; hence, most beloved Advent texts are poetry rather than prose. Advent prophets preach poetry, not because they are fancifully talking about what is not but because they are realistically talking about what is not yet in fullness. We have been so schooled in the limited language of science, government press releases, and subjectivity, so little experienced in poetry, that it is difficult for us to bring to speech that which is large, divine, cosmic. Forgive our prosaic homiletical stammering before the fact of the incarnation. After all, we are attempting to speak of a kingdom so strange and wonderful that only God could have conceived it.

The old world has passed, is passing away before our astonished eyes and a new moral order is being thereby offered. This is not ideal or utopian. It is merely the implication of life in a world that we now, after Bethlehem and Golgotha, know to be *God's* world. Our present is thrown into crisis, even as was Herod's world in crisis "and all Jerusalem with him" (Matt. 2:3). The crisis comes so that the known world can be made new by the gift of possibilities we would not have seen had we not been given this Advent poetic, prophetic light into the future.

It is no surprise that many of our Old Testament texts, coming as they do from Isaiah, will strike a chord with us. These texts come from a time when the Babylonian empire was at the height of its power. Great Nebuchadnezzar (604–562 B.C.E.) was on his throne and all was supposed to be right with the world. Second Isaiah is the literature of a marginalized people whose prophets taught them to dissent from imperial politics. Mark, Luke, and John are all enlisted for Advent/Christmas Gospel texts, texts so diverse yet so similar in having been written during the heyday of imperial Rome when Caesar was on his throne and the whole world was ordered to be at peace.

As long as this people could remember, could sing, and could preach, neither Nebuchadnezzar nor Caesar was safe. Safety, security, respectful deference is not the point of Advent/Christmas.

Our eschatology is, to a great degree, proved by its parochial effects. Christian ethics has its basis in eschatology. A church that envisions a busy, restlessly revolutionary God will make larger moves in its corporate life than a church whose vision of the future has shrunk to the confines of what we can do on our own. "The central task of ministry," says Walter Brueggemann, "is the formation of a community with an alternative, liberated imagination that has the courage and freedom to act in a different vision and a different perception of reality" ("Second Isaiah: An Evangelical Rereading of Communal Experience," in Christopher R. Seitz, ed., *Reading and Preaching the Book of Isaiah* [Philadelphia: Fortress, 1988], 80. Compare with chaps. 3 and 4 of my book, with Stanley Hauerwas, *Resident Aliens: Life in the Christian Colony* [Nashville: Abingdon, 1990]).

Nothing worth saying is timeless, abstracted from a particular context. Therefore, you should know that this volume was written in the summer of 1992, in the context of the Los Angeles riots. These pages ought to smell of the smoke of burning cities, ought to echo the stirrings of restless people on the move.

I heard Rudolph Bohren say, "Preaching which has not continually and restlessly with eschatology to do has not with Christ to do." With that admonition, let us venture into the threatening, untamed Advent wilderness with John, let us plunge into the Baptizer's restless Jordan waters, let us light the torch, let us boldly proclaim, "Prepare the way of the Lord."

Let the revolution begin.

First Sunday in Advent

Lutheran	Roman Catholic	Episcopal	Common Lectionary
Isa. 63:16b-17; 64:1-8	Isa. 63:16b-17, 19b; 64:2b-7	Isa. 64:1-9a	Isa. 63:16—64:8
1 Cor. 1:3-9	1 Cor. 1:3-9	1 Cor. 1:1-9	1 Cor. 1:3-9
Mark 13:33-37	Mark 13:33-37	Mark 13:33-37	Mark 13:32-37

FIRST LESSON: ISAIAH 63:16b-17; 64:1-8

"O that you would tear open the heavens and come down!" (Isa. 64:1). Isaiah 63:16b-17; 64:1-8 is the pushy prayer of a people at the end of their rope, having exhausted all possible human alternatives, having given up on polite, respectfully restrained prayers to God. People on the bottom, people who have lost hope in conventional means of change, do not have the luxury of a deistic "Unmoved Mover," a God who merely sets the world in motion without continued intervention in the world. This prayer names a God who acts. For people at the end of their rope, no less a God could hear or help so no less a God is addressed. Claus Westermann calls this "the most powerful psalm of communal lamentation in the Bible" (*Isaiah 40-66* [Philadelphia: Westminster, 1969], 392).

The preacher may want to explore the metaphor of exile during Advent sermons. As Walter Brueggemann says, "The exile of the contemporary American church is that we are bombarded by definitions of reality that are fundamentally alien to the gospel, definitions of reality that come from the military-industrial-scientific empire. . . . In a variety of ways the voice of this empire wants to reshape our values, fears, and dreams in ways that are fundamentally opposed to the voice of the gospel" ("Second Isaiah," in Seitz, *Reading and Preaching Isaiah*, 73).

Specifically, this is the prayer of those returned from exile, returned to the ruins of the temple and the rubble of defeated national hope (Isa. 63:18). The historical context is that part of Isaiah, so-called Third Isaiah (chaps. 56–66), which struggles with the situation of exile after the fall of Jerusalem in 587 B.C.E. The lectionary's omission of 63:18-19 is unfortunate. Verses 18-19 are evocative images of a people who, having once held the temple, the seat of God's presence, now see the temple in the hands of foreigners. It is as if Israel no longer belongs to God, or even more frightening, as if God no longer belongs to Israel, "like those not called by your name" (v. 19).

9

The prayer moves beyond tearful lament to a bold calling of God to account, reminding the Almighty of divine deeds of deliverance in "ages past" (64:4). Perhaps even more daring is the prayer's ascription of our rebelliousness and hardness to the workings of God (63:17). Somehow, this God is mixed up with the good and the bad, the blessing and the tragedy of life, the broken heart and the hardened heart. Having dared to be monotheists, knowing of no God but one (Deut. 6:4), Israel must follow the implications (troubling though they may be for us polytheists), that all good or ill is somehow related to this one God. These chapters of Isaiah render a God who is so active, alive, and close to us that God is even involved in our ethical straying from God's ways and our political hardness of heart (63:17; compare Deut. 32:39). I agree with David Tracy when he says we need a "re-Judaizing of Christian soteriology against some individualist, ahistorical, and apolitical traditional readings" (Tracy, "Christian Understanding of Salvation-Liberation," 39–40).

Thus our problem with our text from Isaiah is not so much the gap between the originating time of the text and our time, the problem of history, but rather the problem of faith. Dare we pray with Isaiah 63–64 for the advent of a God who "would tear open the heavens and come down"?

Toward the end of one of his movies, Woody Allen says something like, "It's not that I hate God. I have nothing against God. I think that the worst you could say of God is that God is an underachiever." In our minds, God never quite lives up to God's potential.

Note that our lection begins with affirmation that "you are our father" (63:16) and ends with the same acclamation (64:8). The Old Testament has a rich store of images and metaphors for God—the words "for you are our father" occur only here. God as father was a pagan, mythic idea which Israel carefully avoided until rare usages in post-exilic times. In this highly unusual use of the term, the fatherhood of God is presented in terms of our last refuge when even our ancestors no longer know us (63:16). Although our sins are manifold, "*Yet* . . . you are our Father" (64:8). Upon that great, divine, paternal *nevertheless* rests the hope for deliverance in Isaiah 63–64.

It is a fearful thing for a people to arrive at a point in their history where they charge God with having "hidden your face from us" (64:7). Yet even in our hard iniquity, we dare to believe that we are but clay being worked by the formative hands of a skilled potter (64:8). Our hope, at the end of our collective rope, is for the advent of a God who remembers us, even in our forgetfulness of God, and re-forms us into people more worthy to bear the image of the divine. In good or ill, our lives show the thumbprints of the hands of an active God.

GOSPEL: MARK 13:33-37

Pushy, desperate prayer for the advent of God is the proper setting for this Sunday's Gospel, Mark 13:33-37. Within Mark's eschatological discourse (Mark 13:24-37) is set a curious concluding parable. The parable takes place out in Galilee, in a hierarchical world of masters and slaves, of absentee owners and foreign entrepreneurs whose farms are worked by servants who rarely see the boss. This parable is among the familiar departure/return stories (cf. Matt. 24:45-51; Matt. 25:14-30).

The master's departure constitutes a test for the slaves. Having entrusted the slaves with property and responsibility, the master's return will be a time of accounting. Jesus' "It is like a man going on a journey, when he leaves home and puts his slaves in charge" provides the tension within the story (v. 34). The hearer of the parable is led to ask, How well will these slaves perform? What will they do now that the boss is no longer looking over their shoulder? And the master's return is a time of judgment leading the hearer to ask, What will happen when the master shows up?

The master is present, even when he is absent, since it is the master's property and house that the servants are keeping. Yet the master is undeniably absent since it appears that the servants are utterly on their own while the master is away. The master's promised return creates tension within the slaves for they do not know "when the master of the house will come" (v. 35). Often, the boss has a way of showing up at the most inopportune time like "in the evening, or at midnight, or at cockcrow, or at dawn" (v. 35), perhaps in the master's sneaky hope that "he may find you asleep when he comes suddenly" (v. 36).

Slaves with absentee masters must really keep on their toes. Thus the teller of the tale admonishes us, "Keep awake."

Now to whom would this story have been told and to what purpose? Evidently, with its opening editorial admonition to "keep alert," it was told to people who were waiting and were tired of it, people with an absentee master. So much of the New Testament is concerned with the problems generated by an absentee Lord. In one sense, absence can be said to be *the* problem we have with Jesus. The only time we have ever known with him was the time after he had come and gone, time between his first advent and the next. Having experienced Jesus' presence, as the teller of parables, the lord of the banquet, having eaten and drunk with him in the Eucharist, we are all the more pained by his absence. We would not know for what to hope in his second advent, nor would we know how painful is Jesus' absence from us, had we not experienced his full, very real presence among us in his first advent.

It is not merely that our master was once among us but now is absent. It is that Jesus created a particular kind of engaging presence among us so that now, his absence creates a kind of pain that is almost unbearable. Having come so fully among us in Scripture and at the eucharistic table, our time has been forever transformed into his time so that we are never simply without him but we are rather always waiting for him. In Mark's Gospel, Christ's presence provokes an even more profound sense of waiting and yearning.

Like the servants in the parable, the return of the master is a test for us, but not the kind of test where we are expected to have a set of right answers on the tips of our tongues. The master's return is a test in the sense that we be found waiting, between the times, between his first advent and his next, in a way that demonstrates that we know this to be the master's house, and all that we have the master's goods, and our time a time of waiting for the return of the master.

The master has gone. But his departure creates no simple absence. Rather, at his departure the master "puts his slaves in charge, each with his work" (13:34). The work we are left with is the *master's* work so there is plenty to do in the meantime.

The meantime is the only time we have ever known with Jesus, time between his first advent and his next. We have plenty to do, not to work hard to bring in the kingdom through our efforts, but rather to testify, through our efforts, that the kingdom is already present in the advent of Jesus of Nazareth.

This is an important observation for the faithful interpreter of these texts of advent waiting. The interpreter of these texts will want to make clear that we are not talking about any old waiting, any ordinary expectancy. No generalized, existentialized, psychologized sermons on "Expecting the Best of Life," or "Living with Eagerness" can do justice to the eschatological focus of these texts. The God for whose advent Isaiah pleads is not any old God offering any old deliverance. The master for whom the church tensely waits has entrusted to us servants a peculiar property. The time of our waiting is full of particular significance. That significance has a face, Jesus the Christ, a shape, the kingdom of God.

SECOND LESSON: 1 CORINTHIANS 1:3-9

The Gospel parable urges us not to make too much of alleged problems of a "delayed parousia" when reading today's Epistle, 1 Corinthians 1:3-9. Although many in Corinth may have been disappointed that Christ had not returned in the fullness of his power as soon as they had expected, Christ had nevertheless come. 1 Corinthians 1:3-9 addresses an active, busy God. The Corinthian congregation itself is evidence of divine activity.

In his first advent, Christ had brought an end to the world as they had known it. They have received gifts (1:7) and the "fellowship of his Son"

(1:9). Out of nothing, a new world had come into being "because of the grace of God that has been given you in Christ Jesus" (1:4). Although much had changed for the Corinthians in Christ's first advent, not everything had changed. The Corinthians are still a waiting church. All is not well in Corinth, particularly in the church, as we shall learn later in this letter. Thus Paul begins his address to the Corinthians with a prayer, a prayer where we hear echoes of the older prayer of Isaiah 63–64.

"As you wait for the revealing of our Lord Jesus Christ" (1 Cor. 1:7), Paul's encouraging word to the waiting church at Corinth can be our word as well, as we wait. Like the Corinthians, we also need strengthening "to the end" (1:8), reminders of what God has already done among us, encouragement to stand on tiptoes awaiting what else God plans to do with us. Surely this encouragement lies behind all of this First Sunday in Advent's texts—"God is faithful" (1:9).

Considering the congregations where most of us live, we are justified in questioning the wisdom of God's business judgments. Yet today's parable from Mark 13 is quite scandalously clear: In the meantime, God's kingdom has been entrusted to a bunch of servants.

PROCLAIMING THE TEXTS

Sleep is the predominate posture for the church. I first noticed this in the book of Acts. There, some of the most important intrusions of God, such as the revelation to Peter of the inclusiveness of God's kingdom (Acts 10) and the release of Peter from prison (Acts 12), occur while the church and its leaders are fast asleep.

Jesus urged us to stay awake in Gethsemane (Mark 14:32-42), but we fell asleep. Now, on the First Sunday in Advent, the church continues to have difficulty keeping awake. Jesus warns us about God's advent in which "he may find you asleep when he comes suddenly" (Mark 13:36) and urges us to "keep awake" (13:37). It is no accident that Mark has placed this parabolic assault on dormant disciples right before Gethsemane and the cross. As Jesus comes, or as he goes, we are often asleep.

Whenever the master is absent, it is an occasion for a test of the servants.

"Now class, I am going down the hall to the principal's office for a few minutes. I certainly hope that I can trust you to act like responsible fifth graders. But just in case, I'm leaving the door open. I have asked Mrs. Moffat, across the hall, to listen for trouble. I hope that you will show me how responsible you are. I'm leaving now. I had better not hear a word out of you. You have work to do while I am gone. . . ."

It is a worthless servant who can be trusted only when the master is in town. It is an irresponsible class that can be trusted only when the teacher is present.

13

We long for presence, for we are at our best when the master is with us. "Come, Thou Long Expected Jesus" is our advent prayer. "O Come, O Come, Emmanuel" is the advent hymn. "Turn back for the sake of your servants" is our prayer from today's lesson from Isaiah (63:17). "O that you would tear open the heavens and come down" (64:1). When the master is with us, visibly, actively present, we are at our best. When the master is away, things do not always go well. "There is no one who calls on your name . . . for you have hidden your face from us, and have delivered us into the hand of our iniquity" (Isa. 64:7).

We identify with the deep yearning of Isaiah 63–64. The encroaching December dark, the subdued quality of Advent hymns, this morning's headlines all testify to a waiting, unfulfilled world. In the Advent eucharist, we are given bread, but not enough completely to satisfy our hunger, wine, but not enough fully to assuage our thirst. So we light a hopeful candle on the Advent wreath and wait for the coming of the light. It is dark and we fight off the anesthetizing comfort of sleep, feeling that we should be awake, just in case anything happens. It is 3:00 A.M. and we are in the middle of Mark 13:13-37.

Such an interpretation fails to hear the whole claim behind the prayers of Isaiah 63–64, the salutation of 1 Corinthians 1:3-9, or the parable of Mark 13:13-37. Something *has* happened. Isaiah prays for the heavens to be cracked open because the prophet remembers that they have been before. Paul exuberantly addressed the Corinthian church as those who wait, but who have been given much work that whets their appetites for what they wait for.

Mark's parable sets the context for our night vigil. The slaves who wait are those who have met and have known the master. This master is not only a landlord, he is also a wonderfully reckless boss who has "put his slaves in charge, each with his own work" (Mark 13:34).

Everything that the master is and all that he owns has been given to his servants. What sort of master would leave town and place all that he has in the hands of his servants? What sort of servants would be worthy of such trust? "This is my *body*, given for *you*."

I have noted, in my work with students, the best way to make a young person responsible is to give that person great responsibility. I once had a shiftless, half-hearted student, who reluctantly volunteered to be part of a mission work team trip. To my chagrin, his fellow students elected him leader of the team. You know what happened next. He was transformed by their confidence in him, worked day and night (he hardly slept for three weeks!), and led the best team we ever had. The "Therefore keep awake" admonishment of the parable must be read after the "puts his slaves in charge."

We are waiting, this First Sunday in Advent, "for the revealing of our Lord Jesus Christ" (1 Cor. 1:7). But we are not waiting for the advent of a God whom we do not know. We are waiting for the return of the One who knows us and is known by us. His promised kingdom is not a future hope, something that might happen by-and-by. His time is *now*; his kingdom is *here*. Already, he has put his servants in charge, now, each with his work. Now, at the office, in the classroom, over the kitchen sink the master's servants are "in charge, each with his work."

The church gathers this Sunday, lights one candle on a four-candled wreath, blesses the bread and wine in his name, prays, and then trembles upon remembrance. *The kingdom of God has been left in the hands of servants.*

Second Sunday in Advent

Lutheran	Roman Catholic	Episcopal	Common Lectionary
Isa. 40:1-11	Isa. 40:1-5, 9-11	Isa. 40:1-11	Isa. 40:1-11
2 Pet. 3:8-14	2 Pet. 3:8-14	2 Pet. 3:8-15a, 18	2 Pet. 3:8-15a
Mark 1:1-8	Mark 1:1-8	Mark 1:1-8	Mark 1:1-8

FIRST LESSON: ISAIAH 40:1-11

Invariably in the history of God's dealings with us, one can tell whenever God enters the story because suddenly in the text prose gives way to poetry. For most days of our lives, prose is sufficient to the task. Prose is fine for government reports, official decrees, traffic citations, *The New York Times,* and the work of most theologians who are merely systematic.

But just let God intrude into the accustomed flow of things, and prose cracks under the strain. Only poetry can even attempt to speak of what happens when God comes. Only poetry will do.

Alas, for many of us, biblical poetry is a problem to be overcome in order to proclaim the Gospel rather than the normative medium for Gospel proclamation. Luther once said of prophets like Isaiah, "They have a queer way of talking, like people who, instead of proceeding in an orderly manner, ramble off from one thing to the next, so that you cannot make head or tail of them or see what they are getting at" (quoted in Gerhard von Rad, *The Message of the Prophets* [New York: Harper & Row, 1967], 15).

I wonder: Has the eschatological been neglected in our faith in recent centuries (as suggested last Sunday) because many contemporary interpreters of the Christian faith are powerful, affluent and therefore content with the status quo, or because many contemporary interpreters are merely historical critics or theologians rather than poets?

Interpreters have judged Isaiah 40–55 to be so different from the preceding chapters of Isaiah that they have been written by a different hand. The poetry of this "Second Isaiah" quivers with joyful anticipation of deliverance from exile, boldly asserts that even pagan Cyrus has become a tool for the workings of the God of Israel, catches up even the seemingly most secular events of history into a cosmic, divinely ordained plan for God's people. God is doing a new thing before the exile-dulled eyes of Judah and no speech can do justice to the eschatological newness except poetry.

I wonder: Perhaps "Second Isaiah" is "First Isaiah" so close to the threshold of the good news of divine revolution that the writer has been transformed from historian to poet.

This Sunday's first lesson, Isaiah 40:1-11, is the opening movement in a great symphony of divine intervention. Think of this passage as a chorus for four voices:

First, God speaks (Isa. 40:1-2). "Comfort" here is plural imperative. The command to comfort is obeyed, in different ways by the subsequent three voices. Last Sunday's lesson from Isaiah (63:16—64:8) was an anguished cry of the people to God. Today, communication is in the opposite direction. God now speaks, directing affairs, asserting what must be said and how.

Last Sunday, the prophet had asserted that the people's misfortune was the result of their infidelity. Now, their "penalty is paid" (40:2). Note the implicit theodicy here that views all history, both good and ill, as "received from the LORD's hand."

The second voice announces a divine highway construction program. A one-way thoroughfare is to be built, a majestic way back from Babylonian exile whereby "the glory of the LORD shall be revealed" (40:5).

We are surely meant to hear echoes of the Exodus narrative. There, we were in bondage; there, the great, sensitive ears of God heard the liberating cry of the voiceless oppressed, and their God spoke an intruding, liberating promise of deliverance. Comfort must begin with announcement of comfort. In this new exodus out of exile and back home, the whole cosmos shall reflect the good news of return and restoration as once impassable terrain is transformed into a friendly way back home. This exodus, God rules over both the historical and the natural and enlists both politicians like Cyrus as well as the mountains and valleys to serve God's will.

Even though everything in this world decays, fades, and withers, says the third voice, one thing remains: "the word of our God" (40:8).

As a preacher, I have often been impressed with the insubstantial quality of our speech. Words are spoken, they drift out over a listening congregation, echo off walls and ceiling, and die. A sound stirs the air briefly but then is heard no more. Preaching appears to me, a preacher, as the most fragile of the arts. Not here, not in Isaiah 40 (nor in John 1, for that matter). Note that, when all the risings and fallings of history are done, when Second Isaiah's prophecies are fulfilled, the final verses of Second Isaiah (55:10f.) reiterate, reassert that "the word of our God will stand for ever." Thus, Isaiah 40:8 and Isaiah 55:10f. form a frame for an extraordinarily extravagant homiletical claim not believed by many of us, least of all us preachers! Here is a "high" theology of the word.

Even as the word was spoken and a new world was created (Genesis 1), so God's word creates possibility where once there was nothing. Events occur after announcement by the herald (40:3-5, 9), and the news is so good that the preacher is urged to get up on a high mountain to speak (40:9). What is this Isaiah Gospel? "Here is your God!" (40:9).

Poetic metaphor struggles to describe the nature of this divine advent among us. On the one hand it is an event full of "power" and "might" (40:10), on the other hand, "He will feed his flock like a shepherd; he will gather the lambs in his arms, and carry them in his bosom" (40:11). The awesome creator and the gentle shepherd, the paternal and the maternal, the strong and the tender are complementary aspects of this message of comfort and hope being proclaimed to these exiles.

"Here is your God!"

SECOND LESSON: 2 PETER 3:8-15a

Is it any wonder that this promise of God's advent should elicit "scoffers" (2 Peter 3:3), people who mock such eschatological hope saying, "Where is the promise of his coming? . . . all things continue as they were from the beginning of creation!" (2 Peter 3:4)? These are the people who look at human history and see no intrusions, no jolts or surprises that are attributable to God. For them, history is just one thing after another with no real change or newness (compare Eccles. 3:1-9). The old philosopher in Isaac Bashevis Singer's "Pigeons" has much evidence for his assertion that "History is made by the wicked" (*A Friend of Kafka and Other Stories* [New York: Farrar, Straus and Giroux, Inc., 1967]).

Some may think that skepticism is a modern phenomenon, that our trouble with apocalyptic intervention and eschatological claim is recent. This is not true. The author of today's epistle, 2 Peter 3:8-15a, realizes that skepticism, which presents itself as the fruit of a sophisticated, intellectual mind, is more often the sad result of a mind that is too small. Faith is more a matter of imagination than blind belief. Our senses have been dulled by the everyday. Our vision is limited to our own personal experience so we measure time with teaspoons. "With the Lord . . . a thousand years are like one day" (3:8). What some scoffers may regard as divine immobility is the result, not of slowness, but of the patience of a God who is willing to wait until we at last come to our senses and repent (3:9).

Furthermore, all those seemingly so substantial elements to which we cling, on whose deludingly concrete reality we base our skepticism—the good, solid stuff of life like money, government, culture—"will be dissolved with fire" (3:10). In this great, final, cosmic, divinely ordained meltdown, we shall see how insubstantial were the matters to which we ascribed eternal value, how our efforts to "save the planet," or to save our own skins were pitifully inept in the face of the next flood of judgment.

Thus the writer of 2 Peter calls listeners to an act of prophetic imagination, urges us to take the long view whereby we see those things that endure and those things that do not, thus echoing the theme of Isaiah 40:6-8. The people, grass, flowers, all pass away, but "the word of our God will stand forever" (40:8).

Odd that such apocalyptic thought should be accused by later interpreters of undercutting the ethical with pie-in-the-sky futuristic escapism. If we have learned one thing from a century of biblical criticism, it is that the Christian message is utterly eschatological. In fact, the Christian message is ethical because it is eschatological, as 2 Peter 3:11-14 makes explicit: "Since all these things are to be dissolved in this way, what sort of persons ought you to be . . . ?" (3:11).

The prophetic is a by-product of the apocalyptic. A friend of mine was talking to a pastor in the Latvian Methodist Church shortly after Christians in Latvia were given their freedom to again practice their religion after years of horrible persecution by the Communists. The pastor excitedly reported the amazing, almost overnight explosion of the church in Latvia.

"How on earth did you manage to keep your faith?" asked my friend.

"Well, we always took the long view," replied the pastor. "We only had sixty years to wait, this time. We took the long view."

Apocalyptic speech will cause difficulty for a church that clings too tightly to present power arrangements, which expends too much intellectual energy defending the way things are and too little expectantly awaiting how, by God's grace, things might be. Scoffers of every age base their objections to apocalyptic, prophetic poetry on a variety of accusations— it is naive, premodern, unrealistic. Believers respond with 2 Peter that apocalyptic requires a great deal of holy imagination.

GOSPEL: MARK 1:1-8

How fitting that today's Gospel should be that wonderfully weird prophetic herald of change, John the Baptist. Like Isaiah 40, John announces cosmic newness, first things through a new word (compare John 1:1-3). He does so in Mark 1:2b-3 through a composite of beloved passages from the Hebrew Scriptures (Exod. 23:20, Mal. 3:1, and yes, Isa. 40:3). Past, pushy, poetic, prophetic voices are heard again in the preaching of John. John is thus a transition figure, a prophet standing somewhere on the boundary between prophets past and the present good news of Jesus Christ. He is like a herald, sent to announce the arrival of the king, an emissary whose appearance signals the inauguration of a new kingdom. This "beginning of the good news" is the beginning of a new age.

Poetic images are loaded onto one another in Mark's description of the message of John. John prepares the way (1:2), cries from the wilderness that the wilderness is about to be subdued and civilized by a coming Lord (1:3). As sign of this radical newness, John calls everyone to get washed, cleaned, ready. He invites all to "a baptism of repentance for the forgiveness of sins" (1:4). Repentance means a reorientation of one's life, a fresh start, metamorphosis. John calls people out from the grip of the empire and into the wilderness, beckons them to pass through the waters of a new Red Sea, to begin again a new exodus, *metanoia*. John tells people that he comes washing with the water of baptism but there is one who is coming next who shall pour out the Holy Spirit. Water for cleansing, holy breath for new life—John promises that we shall be clean and that we shall be able to breathe again (1:8).

John's message is called good news because it is news of change, of new beginning and a fresh start due to the advent of "one who is more powerful than I" (1:7). John's sermon, much shorter than the more detailed sermons reported by Matthew (3:1-12) and Luke (3:1-20), is meant to be evocative, is meant to leave the listener asking, "Who is this mighty one who comes, one whose baptism shall bring such newness?"

It would be appropriate this Second Sunday of Advent if our sermon left our congregations asking that baptismal question.

PROCLAIMING THE TEXTS

In Handel's *Messiah* there comes that point where the tenor stands, and with clear, clean voice announces, "Comfort ye, comfort ye, my people." The world rustles with expectation upon hearing such a voice. Ears perk up. We are waiting, this Second Sunday in Advent, for a voice to announce that expectation is about to become fulfillment, that the one for whom we have been waiting is about to knock at the door.

"The beginning of the good news of Jesus Christ," says Mark (1:1). The beginning of the gospel is a word, an announcement. Mark's word is so new that Mark must invent a new literary construction (a "gospel") to speak it, so new that no conventional personality can speak it. No one less strange than John the Baptist is up to delivering such good news.

The news is good because it is an address to human pain and yearning; it is news because nothing within conventional human experience prepares us for the peculiar quality of this divine intrusion in Jesus. Only one who both knows firsthand the nature of our yearning, and who knows firsthand the peculiar news of the gospel (someone like an average parish pastor) is fit to deliver this prophetic, evangelical announcement, "Prepare the way of the Lord."

Perhaps that voice is yours.

The one who proclaims this news might first note our innate cynicism and skepticism about the possibility of newness. Today's Epistle, 2 Peter

3:8-14, might be the place to begin. We believe that we know what we have experienced and because we have experienced few divine intrusions, we naturally tend toward skepticism. In the death of eschatological expectation is the death of hope and in the death of hope is the demise of Christian ethics. Rather than make big moves, we relax, settle into present arrangements, old habits, circular movements. We cling tightly to what is rather than dare to dream about what ought to be.

Yet even within our limited contemporary experience, we do know enough about intrusion, intervention, and newness to resonate to the eschatological poetry of Isaiah 40 or to the preaching of John the Baptist. Even the most complacent mind remembers the birth of a child, the new life after successful surgery, what it feels like to at last be free of some old, destructive habit, the first day of school in the fall, the life-changing meeting with God at the altar. Not all may know the fullness of our cosmic, eschatological Christian hope, but everyone knows what it means to bathe, to emerge fresh and clean and ready for a new day. Let the preacher link with these ordinary human experiences of newness and change in order to move us toward the wider baptismally derived hope for Advent proclaimed in today's texts.

It has been a tradition of the church to focus upon Scripture and the Word during this Second Sunday of Advent. Isaiah's "the word of our God will stand forever" (40:8) invites comment on the interplay between proclamation, announcement, preaching, and our Advent hope. The Word creates newness, space, possibility in the desert, a path from God to us. The Word not only describes the world, but offers a new world. We preachers create a world through our words. Let us take our cue from communicators like Isaiah and John and make evocation rather than description the goal of our Second Sunday of Advent speaking.

Appropriate pre-sermon questions for the preacher might be: What are some of the largest moves you have made in your own life? What were the conditions whereby you changed? What is the road God is building toward you today? What did you need to hear before you could change? What is there about us that makes us feel threatened by newness? Are we really so tied to old ways, so in need of metamorphosis that we must strip down, dive in, and be washed?

Preacher, watch your language this Sunday. Let your diction match that of Second Isaiah, of whom Claus Westermann says, "His language is from first to last evocative, arousing, even insistent—witness the way in which he piles imperative on imperative. . . . It was the way he adopted to speak to [people] whose faith was flagging, and who were at the point of letting themselves drift . . . when their observance of traditional usage had no power to lead them to expect any new thing from their God" (*Isaiah 40–66*, 6).

Third Sunday in Advent

Lutheran	Roman Catholic	Episcopal	Common Lectionary
Isa. 61:1-3, 10-11	Isa. 61:1-2a, 10-11	Isa. 65:17-25	Isa. 61:1-4, 8-11
1 Thess. 5:16-24	1 Thess. 5:16-24	1 Thess. 5:16-28	1 Thess. 5:16-24
John 1:6-8, 19-28	John 1:6-8, 19-28	John 1:6-8, 19-28	John 1:6-8, 19-28

Her question seemed so right, so disarmingly to the point, that I could not get rid of it. "How dare you," she asked at the end of our celebration of the eucharist, "speak of joy and gladness when there are hungry people in the world?"

If you want a question to keep in mind as we listen to this Sunday's texts, let it be that. *How dare we, in a suffering, hurting world, rejoice?*

FIRST LESSON: ISAIAH 61:1-3, 10-11

Today is the church's old *Gaudete* Sunday, a one Sunday respite of joy halfway through Advent. For a time, the church stressed Advent as a penitential season, time for sackcloth and ashes, introspection, confession, purple on the altar. Today Isaiah bids us to exchange our sackcloth and ashes for garlands and festive garments, to move from penance to eucharist, to trade in our mourning for gladness, to dress the altar in light, Advent blue, and in general, "to bring good news to the oppressed," even if we don't feel like it.

Of course, in the matter of divinely initiated, exuberant, revolutionary joy, our feelings have little to do with it. Here is joy that derives not from a positive psychological assessment of ourselves (self-esteem) but rather because God has intruded, causing Israel's "righteousness and praise to spring up before all the nations" (61:11).

In Isaiah 61:1-3, the prophet is given God's spirit in order to have the voice to herald jubilee (see Exod. 23:11; Deut. 15:1-5). Almost anyone can bring bad news. Bad news, because there is so much of it, comes quite naturally to speech. It takes spirit (61:1) to bring good news. And here, the good news is explicitly political—food, health, and opening of jails (61:1-3).

It does not really matter that Israel's prophesied jubilee year may have never been put into actual practice. What matters is that Israel knew that a year of reversal of fate was demanded and expected by God. Jubilee was a time of restoration and restitution when the poor would be lifted up and the hungry would be fed. The proclamation of jubilee meant that no present social arrangement could claim divine legitimacy for itself, no system of economic distribution or power-sharing that was less than jubilee (and aren't they all?) could claim exemption from prophetic criticism and prophetic change. No time less than jubilee time was "the year of the LORD's favor" (61:2).

It was precisely in this act of prophetic remembrance and proclamation that Israel displayed the true glory of God (61:3). A people who have no means of measurement beyond the present moment, outside the bounds of its own subjective notions of righteousness, is dangerous. Jubilee kept hope alive, made social self-criticism possible, offered an alternative to present arrangements. Isaiah, as usual, speaks poetically of this alternative reality. A vast symbolic exchange occurs: garlands for ashes, healing oil instead of mourning, protective mantles rather than fainting spirit (61:3). Any large social movement is energized by an exchange of metaphor. I stood before the Lincoln memorial as Martin Luther King, Jr. took us with him up the mountaintop to survey a new world larger than our segregated arrangements. Don't tell me, a South Carolina native, that dreams do not come true. King bid us to dream our way into a new way of being together. Change is impossible while old metaphors grip our lives.

And yes, there is no significant change without some pain. The jubilee time of joyous restoration is also "the day of vengeance of our God" (61:2). Vengeance for what? We are not told. Certainly, as Mary knew (Luke 1:46-55), it is impossible to lift up the lowly without a put-down of the mighty. When the hungry are filled with good things, the rich go away empty. Is this exchange of power and ruling metaphor what Isaiah means by "the day of vengeance of our God"?

But mostly there is joy: "I will greatly rejoice in the LORD, my whole being shall exult in my God" (61:10). The dusty, frayed clothing of the downtrodden is exchanged for "garments of salvation" (61:10), as a bride and a groom dress up for their wedding day. Third Isaiah is the prophet of joy. When exiles return home (40:9), Zion is a place of unceasing celebration. The salvation party extends to the whole neighborhood (42:11f.), the whole earth, to the sea and its teaming creatures (42:10f.). Even the mountains and trees are caught up in the ecological merriment and laughter (44:23; 49:13; 55:12).

Claus Westermann notes that Hebrew has no word for the anticipation of joy, for looking forward to happiness. In the Hebrew, "joy" or "rejoicing" is always and everywhere in direct reaction to something that happens. Joy is reflexive, responsive. "Behold, I bring you good tidings of great joy" (Luke 2:10).

Once again we note that Isaiah has no expectation that his people will play an active role in what is about to happen. This joy is not self-induced. Joy is the fruit of a God who acts: "The Lord GOD will cause righteousness and praise to spring up before all the nations" (61:11).

All the other nations, looking on, clutching their sober, melancholy gods, shall see what a real God can do, shall hear the raucous celebration all the way up in Babylon. Thus, Israel, made righteous, shall display the glory of a just and loving God (61:3).

GOSPEL: JOHN 1:6-8, 19-28

Having been introduced to John the Baptist last Sunday in Mark 1:1-8, we may have a rather negative first impression of him. There the Baptizer's clothing, eating habits, and message are somewhat forbidding. John's John the Baptist is the same transitional prophet as Mark's, but his sermon now sounds different. Whereas Mark says the Baptizer's sermons were about "repentance for the forgiveness of sins" (Mark 1:4), John's Baptizer is "a witness to testify to the light" (John 1:6). If the Messiah is the one who comes to throw a great party for all of Israel's dispossessed (Isaiah 40), then John delivers the invitation. The true light is on its way to enlighten a dismal world (John 1:9).

Some bigwigs are dispatched from the authorities in Jerusalem to investigate the baptismal commotion in the hinterland. "Who are you?" they ask (John 1:19), inquiring into John's credentials, his pedigree, his authority for causing a ruckus among the people. A wonderfully funny quiz ensues. "Are you Elijah?" Elijah had a way of stirring things up when he was with us. *No.* "A prophet?" Prophets have always had a nasty disrespect for propriety, boundaries, rules. *No.* "Then *who are you?*" The thought police, the keepers of law and order, the media moguls downtown want to know!

John answers by quoting last Sunday's lection from Isaiah 40. He is not the long-awaited one. He is the herald, the witness to the arrival of the long-awaited one. He calls people to get washed, clean, fresh, ready to party.

This John who so quickly arouses the suspicion of the authorities is neither Messiah, nor the light, nor Elijah, nor one of the prophets. In fact, in John's Gospel, we are given little help in deciphering *who* John is: no clothing, diet, and only a snippet of his sermon. He is, by his own admission, "a voice," an intruding, disrupting, joy-eliciting prophetic voice. John is the voice we have learned to love in Isaiah. John's main vocation here is that of a voice, a voice that denies any special accolade, a voice that is determined not to block access to the One whom the voice announces, a voice who desires to be "witness to the light."

In Mark, John speaks about the differences between his baptism and that of the one who comes after him (Mark 1:8). Here, in John's Gospel, John's baptism is testimony to the One who stands among us "whom you do not know" (1:26).

Groping to know who it is whom the herald announces, we are given precious little to go on at this point in the Advent story. We know that John is "not the light" (1:8), that John's testimony is also a denial (1:20-21). The Fourth Gospel is intent right at the beginning—here in Advent, before we ever meet the Christ, "The Word"—in insisting that we must abandon our previously conditioned expectations, our conventional categories, in order to greet the "one whom you do not know" (1:26).

Here, as we wait in Advent darkness, here amid the clamor of a waiting world all too willing to throw a Christmas party for a host of yuletide gods of greed and sentiment, let us pause to ponder the warning of the Baptizer. We do not know the one whom we await. Perhaps the path being made straight in the wilderness (1:23) does not lead toward the gods on whom we wait. Some new face peers out at us, from the darkness, standing behind John, coming after the Baptizer, One whom we do not know. Is the commotion, the advent, the eschatological commotion caused by John's voice leading us toward "the year of the LORD's favor" or to "the day of vengeance of our God" (Isaiah 61:2)? We must yet wait. We do not know.

SECOND LESSON: 1 THESSALONIANS 5:16-24

The sobering note on which we end our encounter with this Sunday's Gospel suggests that if this is truly "Joy Sunday," and, if the Advent of God's Messiah elicits joy from us captives who wait, it must be no simple joy. If we do not know the One who comes (John 1:26), do we also not know the peculiar joy produced by His arrival?

Perhaps such theological analysis is meant to be laid aside by the time the church gathers on *Gaudete*, the Third Sunday in Advent. We accept Isaiah's invitation to "proclaim the year of the LORD's favor" (Isa. 61:2) and follow Paul's call to "Rejoice always, pray without ceasing, give thanks in all circumstances" (1 Thess. 5:16-18).

Here, between Christ's first advent and the next, it is possible to lose heart, to become cynical, to allow mourning, ashes, and "a faint spirit" to consume us (Isa. 61:3). How is it possible to rejoice, to greet "all circumstances" with thanksgiving? Such joy is impossible, or simple self-delusion were it not for our faith that "the one who calls you is faithful, and he will do this" (1 Thess. 5:24).

Robin Scroggs notes that Paul really saw the church as living in a new world:

> The act of God in Christ has done more than merely acquaint the sinner; it has created the possibility of living in a new world, radically different from the culture of sin and death. And this possibility is not reserved, postponed, for the future; it is a present possibility which Paul sees actually realized in the church. (*Paul for a New Day* [Philadelphia: Fortress, 1977], 182)

Far from being infatuated with a problem of postponement, Scroggs sees Paul struggling with pastoral/ecclesial enactment: "eschatological selfhood is the return, the restoration to original, authentic, human reality. The way ahead, into eternal life, thus turns out to be the way back, the restoration to creational humanity as designed by God" (*Paul for a New Day*, 156). And that is why there is joy.

Thus we return to Isaiah's announcement of good news, the Baptist's testimony to the light in Paul's admonition to a waiting church not to "quench the Spirit" (1 Thess. 5:19). With garlands, festive garments, and promise of a great, national party, Advent prophets bid us to lay aside our doubts, to be washed, made ready to join the great Feast of the Incarnation, the dawn of our Light, the "coming of our Lord Jesus Christ" (1 Thess. 5:23). Let us not quench the Spirit.

PROCLAIMING THE TEXTS

A witness testifies to something that has been heard and seen. The court is uninterested in the personality or life history of the witness. Even the character of the witness is unimportant except that the witness be honest enough to testify to what the witness has seen and heard.

John the Baptist, at least in John's introduction of him in today's Gospel, is intent on convincing us that "he himself was not the light, but he came to testify to the light" (John 1:8).

In recent years, we preachers have been encouraged do "share your story," to expose ourselves and our struggles to the gaze of the congregation, to preach "inductively," inviting the congregation to link its experience with our personal experience in democratically shared conversation. The preacher's task is to evoke from within us what we already know. (See my criticism of inductive preaching in *Peculiar Speech: Preaching to the Baptized* [Nashville: Abingdon, 1992], chap. 2.)

Little in this Sunday's texts supports such preaching. Isaiah's captives are too down, too bound, too gripped by imperial powers to be expected to free themselves by themselves. Only a God who anoints, sends, binds up, releases, comforts, gives, and invites can help these people (Isa. 61:1-3, 10-11). The Baptizer's Jordan congregation is too tied to old configurations of power, old officially sanctioned readings of the texts, to see anything new without the aid of light. They do not already know the one to whom the Baptist testifies.

First Church Thessalonia is growing too tired of waiting, has had too many false starts, to celebrate anything less than the advent of a God who is both faithful and active. Perhaps that is why there is so little real joy in our congregations. If we do experience joy, it is too often the ersatz high of a merely emotional rush brought on by an effective music program—joy induced by a pleasing soprano voice backed up by a pre-recorded tape. If the only theology we have to preach is of the pull-yourself-up-by-your-bootstraps variety, then we are doomed. Doom produces gloom. In our better moments, we know that the ultimate sources of our mourning are more than psychological—they are political, social, maybe even cosmic. This society tries to convince us that if we are hungry for something more than food, if we gaze at the full shop windows at Christmas and can't find anything we really want, if we wander through the decorated shopping malls in a daze, it is a personal problem, something amiss in our psyche, something in need of corrective therapy.

What if, as Isaiah implies, our problem is as much political as psychological? What if what's wrong with us is what's wrong in the whole society, something out of kilter in the cosmos? What if our pain will be soothed by nothing less than the advent of God? The offer of anything less is a cheap substitute, a set-up for even greater despair. Real, full-throated, full-orbed, let loose joy is a gift to those who have heard the testimony: *Our God comes*.

This returns us to the question with which we began this *Gaudete* Sunday encounter with Advent texts: How dare we, in a suffering, hurting world rejoice?

The question has within itself an answer. *Dare* is the right word to characterize this Sunday's service. If we Christians are joyful, ours is not the simple-minded, bubble-brained cheerfulness of those who deny the world's hunger and pain or who think that somehow, it is all for the best. Joy is to us a gift, a Christmas gift of a God who is never content to leave us be, who intrudes, offers, creates. The typical response to mourning is speechlessness. We become so hurt we cannot speak. We dare not speak for fear that we may make the pain worse.

But sometimes the Spirit intrudes, anoints us to speak, gives voice to a joy not of our own creation. Sometimes a light surprises our all-too-accustomed darkness and, for the first time in a long time, we see. Sometimes we experience so much of the near presence of God that we never stop rejoicing, prayer becomes like breathing, and even in the worst of circumstances, we dare to give thanks.

Dare to believe it possible. "The one who calls you is faithful, and he will do this" (1 Thess. 5:24).

"Blessed are you who are poor, for yours is the kingdom of God. Blessed are you who are hungry now, for you will be filled" (Luke 6:20-21).

The King is coming, the table is being prepared (Luke 19:37-38).

Rejoice.

Fourth Sunday in Advent

Lutheran	Roman Catholic	Episcopal	Common Lectionary
2 Sam. 7:1-11, 16	2 Sam. 7:1-5, 8b-12, 14a, 16	2 Sam. 7:4, 8-16	2 Sam. 7:8-16
Rom. 16:25-27	Rom. 16:25-27	Rom. 16:25-27	Rom. 16:25-27
Luke 1:26-38	Luke 1:26-38	Luke 1:26-38	Luke 1:26-38

FIRST LESSON: 2 SAMUEL 7:1-16

Here, as Advent draws to a close and our hopes reach fulfillment, it is well that today's texts have us ponder the peculiar nature of the fulfillment offered to us in the incarnation. All of this Sunday's lessons speak of fulfillment, but all of them mean to rearrange, reread, and dislocate our expectations.

2 Samuel 7:1-16 is a debate between the two kings, Yahweh and David, about suitable housing for royalty. If we have been singing, "Come, O come, Immanuel, and ransom captive Israel," we shall want to be attentive to this debate over royal quarters. Also, because homelessness is much on our minds—widespread homelessness generated by our economy and the way we have chosen to manage it—and also the promise of housing, a home is a promise to which we must attend.

David, through the prophet Nathan, has a proposal for Yahweh. David proposes, in an act of royal generosity, to build a suitable "house" for Yahweh, a temple fitting for the house of a God of a soon-to-be great nation like Israel. "The LORD is with you," says Nathan, thus giving the divine permission for the project (7:3). Upon further reflection, the prophet Nathan hears a reversal of these plans. Now he says, "The LORD will make *you* a house" (7:11). If any "houses" are to be built, if any dynasties are to be established, Yahweh will do the building and the establishing. Perhaps we are reading here a critique of our definitions of royalty, our conceptions of power. The text begins, "when the king was settled in his house" (7:1). David feels that he is now "settled," that he is now secure from the assaults of his enemies with peace and prosperity just around the corner. Now, set up in his elegant new house of cedar, the king decides that he will provide suitable housing for God.

What first appears to be a clear act of royal generosity is more ambiguous than we thought. David, as a new oriental potentate, needs a God commensurate with his newly achieved power. A king is measured by the sort of God who is his patron. This great house for God is perhaps only an extension of the king's great plans for himself.

Yahweh is not impressed, seems to have no need to settle down and be domesticated in Israel. The Lord addresses the king as "*my servant* David" (7:4), asking him, "Are you the one to build me a house to live in?" (7:5). The king may need a house to shore up his reign, but not Yahweh. Yahweh has been roaming about, on the move "in a tent and a tabernacle" (7:6) since he adopted Israel. Yahweh sneeringly asks, "Why have you not built me a house of cedar?" (7:7).

Now follows a whole series of statements in the divine first person singular, "I took you. . . . I have been with you. . . . I have cut off all your enemies. . . . I will make you. . . . I will appoint a place for my people. . . ." (7:8-10). The action has shifted from what the king plans to do to a reminder of all that Yahweh has done, thus subtly asking us to rearrange our ideas of who is really king here. If any establishment of kingly houses is to be done here, it will be done by Yahweh, not by David.

Here, our text manages both to promise the establishment of a house and a throne forever (7:16), as well as to critique the notion of royal power. This kingdom, this Israel, will not be established by King David and his plans, accomplishments, and public works programs; rather, Yahweh shall establish Israel. 2 Samuel 7:8-16 is the foundational document for the messianic hopes of Israel, for the revival of David's rule after the fall of Jerusalem in 587 B.C.E. Yet within the hope is a critique of the hope. Within the expectation is a warning against false messianic expectation. Within the establishment of a king is a deconstruction of who kings are and from whence their power is derived.

David seeks a house, a home for himself and his aspirations. Yahweh is the giver of houses, the maker of a home "sure forever" (7:16). Let us note along with the affirmation is an Advent caveat: Yahweh's homemaking and house-building may be different from our own. Here we have been in Advent, preparing to build God a house, a home in our hearts. But this God won't be taken in by us, won't be tamed and housebroken. Yahweh builds us a home. Let us mark well this debate over true kingship and thereby be prepared to be surprised by the nature of the reign which is being born among us.

SECOND LESSON: ROMANS 16:25-27

Our second lesson is a doxology and is therefore more appropriately sung than analyzed. After having just read today's first lesson from 2 Samuel, we are impressed that this doxology begins, as doxology usually does, with ascription "to God who is able to strengthen you" (16:25). The strengthening promised is not for self-esteem, or material prosperity, or happiness, or most of the other goods we desire at this time of year, but rather for "my Gospel and the proclamation of Jesus Christ" (16:25). The content of "my Gospel" can be discerned only by reference to the preceding chapters of Paul's letter to the Romans. Here is a large, demanding, exuberant Gospel, the reception of which is impossible without divine strengthening. Once again, as in our first lesson, the initiative, that which is being offered, is God and not ourselves.

Here is a high theology of God's nature, a God who has something in store even for "all the Gentiles" (16:26). This great, divine plan was "kept secret for long ages but is now disclosed" (16:25-26) says Paul. Advent is the breaking open—the making visible, incarnate of God's great, mysterious plan. We are fortunate to be able to be living in such days, says Paul. No wonder we sing.

"These are the days of miracle and wonder," sings Paul Simon in his song, "The Boy in the Bubble" on his *Graceland* album. The words speak of "The way we look to a distant constellation / That's dying in a corner of the sky" and tells us that "This is the long-distance call." The apocalyptic words were called to my attention by a student who is an aficionado of contemporary music. I hear them as an echo of our song in Romans 16:25-27. Our age of "miracle and wonder" is too often "Medicine is magical and magical is art / The boy in the bubble / And the baby with the baboon heart." That's the closest we come to real mystery and wonder. So Paul Simon counsels us, "Don't cry baby, don't cry / Don't cry."

St. Paul is talking about some other kind of apocalyptic, although it is interesting that Paul Simon knows that our age can only be adequately described by apocalyptic speech of some sort. By the way, I asked the student who put me on to "The Boy in the Bubble" to make me a list of any other contemporary songs that used apocalyptic imagery. Within a few minutes he had thought of over thirty.

We long to be the recipients of a "long-distance call." When we receive such a call, Paul says we sing.

GOSPEL: LUKE 1:26-38

After all of this Advent talk of kings, power, thrones, and royalty, we have been perfectly set up by the preceding texts to be shocked by the Gospel. 2 Samuel has promised us the establishment of a dynasty that "shall be established forever" (2 Sam. 7:16). Paul has invited us to sing about the disclosure of "the mystery that was kept secret for long ages" (Rom. 16:25). And who is the source of this dynasty, this great mystery of all the ages? A poor, pregnant, peasant girl named Mary living in a dusty town named Nazareth (Luke 1:26-38).

Luke carefully links Mary "to a man whose name was Joseph, of the house of David," thus signaling a connection between this upcoming birth and the messianic expectation of 2 Samuel 7:1-11, 16. But nothing in Mary's demeanor or circumstances fits our conventional expectations for royalty and royal power.

We are further surprised when the angel, this divine messenger, addresses Mary as if she were a queen, "Greetings, favored one! The Lord is with you" (Luke 1:28). Yet Mary is just as confused as we are and wonders "what sort of greeting this might be" (1:29).

Earlier, in the very text establishing the eternal "house of David" (2 Sam. 7:10-16) we were told that Yahweh doesn't need a palace, a fine house, a throne. Yahweh is free to roam. Now we find that this peripatetic God has roamed down to Nazareth, way down to a peasant house, to a poor woman named Mary.

As Mary is left, here on the eve of the incarnation, to ponder "what sort of greeting this might be," so are we. Earlier, God talked to David through the medium of the prophet Nathan (2 Sam. 7:2-16). Now God communicates directly to lowly Mary through his chosen emissary, the angel Gabriel (Luke 1:26). All of this is meant to rearrange our images of who God is, where God works. Here is a king who is busy, not up at the palace with kings, but down in the ghetto with the meek and lowly. Earlier, David was this king's servant, the one who had been chosen to do Yahweh's bidding. Now a woman, a peasant woman, Mary from Nazareth is the one being enlisted for the final, ultimate fulfillment of the promised establishment of a throne that shall last forever and a kingdom and a rule without end.

Just by telling the story, simply by listening to the story, we are receiving revelation, a mystery is being disclosed to us: The hiddenness of God— hidden not because of God's secrecy but rather because of our own lack of imagination and fidelity—is being revealed to us.

Now is the time to light the fourth and last candle on the Advent wreath. Having had our gaze redirected from the palace, from the centers of power and management, turned now toward the ghetto, toward the small town, the little people, women like Mary, we are now ready to celebrate the new reign.

PROCLAIMING THE TEXTS

There is a tension beneath our texts on this Fourth Sunday of Advent, a tension that we may characterize as a dilemma about which liturgical color, Advent purple or Advent blue, belongs on our altar this Sunday.

Recent liturgical innovations have urged blue as the color of Advent. There is much to be said for Advent blue on the altar. The accustomed purple, often associated with Lent and penitence, risks transforming Advent into a kind of pre-Christmas Lent, a time for sackcloth and ashes before fruitcake and Christmas finery, a time for homiletical scolding and moralizing.

Not wanting that, we turn to blue, the color of the sky when the light has come, the blue of dawn. Blue is traditionally Mary's color and this Sunday's Gospel is her story.

Yet purple is more widely recognized as the color of royalty than the color of penitence. Today's first lesson is about royalty, so is today's Psalm, Psalm 89. These lessons make clear that Advent is about the welcome of a king, the displacement of one configuration of power by another. There is something to be said for purple, color of royalty.

Of course, royal images must be used with care by the biblical preacher. The king and the temple are deeply problematic figures in the history of Israel. David's dynasty was a decidedly mixed phenomenon for Israel; his son Solomon's reign, foretold in today's first lesson, was even more so.

Royal images are therefore not simply transposed from the Old Testament into the New. In the story of the annunciation to Mary, our images of royalty are being rearranged. Yet, as we noted in our discussion of the first lesson from 2 Samuel, images of royalty, human and divine, the nature of rule and kingship, are also being reworked in 2 Samuel.

Rather than fix our gaze upon the alleged humility of Mary, her traditional docility and acquiescence to the mysterious workings of God in her, perhaps we ought to recover the image of Mary, Queen of Heaven. In this woman from Nazareth, old configurations of power, once so fixed and closed, appear to be shifting, deconstructing. The preacher would therefore do well to ask, in preparation for the sermon, Who is benefiting from these shifts of power and who will pay? If Mary is the prefigurement of the new reign, what are the contours of that reign? What can we expect from a kingdom that is established in this way?

The first lesson puts kings, royalty, rule, and power on the table for discussion. Today's Gospel continues, rearranges, enlarges that discussion by shifting it to Mary's neighborhood, a peculiar locale for traditional messianic expectations. We are claiming here that the prophetic promise of Nathan, "the LORD will make you a house" (2 Sam. 7:11), is being fulfilled. But look where the "house" is being built.

Of course there are many who say that royal images of kings, thrones, power, and rule are too corrupted by dominant imperial ideology to be reconstructed by us Christian preachers. Noting the tragic consequences when these images have been misconstrued as a call to quietism, passivity, and false hopes, they tell us preachers to leave behind royal metaphors as something we have at last outgrown. But I bid you to put purple on the altar and prepare to welcome a new king, preparing also, with the help of Scripture, to be prepared to be shocked by the king we are given.

A year or so ago, Thailand was rocked by civil unrest in which the people filled the streets to protest a military government's installation of a prime minister who was not elected by the people. The government reacted with a brutal massacre of the unarmed protestors. Days of riots, destruction, and chaos followed. The people refused to relent and to return to their homes, the government refused to give in to the people's demands. At last the beloved king of Thailand called the disputed prime minister and the leader of the opposition to his palace. In deference to the king, to centuries of tradition, and popular affection for him, they both meekly knelt before him. The king ordered the two parties to stop fighting, end the violence, and work things out. In less than a day, the disturbances were over, the ersatz prime minister was on his way out of the country, and peace was restored.

One news commentator said, "The events in Thailand this week are a great victory of democracy." I, schooled by texts like 2 Samuel 7:1-11, 16 and Luke 1:26-38 called it a great victory for monarchy.

There is much to be said, particularly for those on the bottom, for royalty. It all depends upon who is the king who comes. My friend, Stanley Hauerwas, was once asked by one of his disbelieving colleages, "Who wants a God who punishes, who 'Casts the mighty down from their thrones and sends the rich empty away' "? [quoting Mary's battle song in Luke 1:46-55]. Who would want a God of wrath and vengeance who makes war on kings, punishes those who have too much food, and scatters the proud?" Hauerwas answered, "Who wants that kind of God? *The poor.*"

The Nativity of Our Lord, 1
The Service at Night

Lutheran	Roman Catholic	Episcopal	Common Lectionary
Isa. 9:2-7	Isa. 9:2-7	Isa. 9:2-4, 6-7	Isa. 9:2-7
Titus 2:11-14	Titus 2:11-14	Titus 2:11-14	Titus 2:11-14
Luke 2:1-20	Luke 2:1-14	Luke 2:1-14	Luke 2:1-20

FIRST LESSON: ISAIAH 9:2-7

What sort of people would turn over the reins of government to a baby?

We shall sidestep the historian's rather pointless speculation that perhaps these lines were written for the coronation, or anniversary of the coronation, of King Hezekiah, whose rule began in Jerusalem around 720 B.C.E. Instead, we shall struggle to read this text typologically, as weird politics that can only be explained if read backwards, back from Jesus' birth to enlighten this beautiful and obscure passage from Isaiah. We shall therefore assume that Handel (in *Messiah*) knew much more about this passage than von Rad.

The poetry is for "people who walked in darkness," people in Soweto, Bosnia-Herzegovina, Belfast, and certain portions of Detroit or Los Angeles. Verses 2–5 are almost exclusively drawn from the battlefield— speaking of plunder, yokes, rods, boots, and blood. Not exactly what one expects to hear at church on Christmas.

The text's answer to this battlefield horror is astonishing. "For a child has been born for us, a son given to us; authority rests upon his shoulders" (9:6). Every exuberant acclamation is heaped upon this child who is named "Wonderful Counselor, Mighty God, Everlasting Father, Prince of Peace" (9:6).

How can this be? How can a mere baby be the answer to what ails us? What good is a baby toddling amid battlefield ruin? Whose idea of politics is this?

The answer is in the last verse of tonight's text: "The zeal of the LORD of hosts will do this" (9:7). The Lord, always so full of political surprises, has bushwacked us with a baby.

So accustomed are we to think pejoratively of "zeal," so frightened have we become, in our tame religion, of "zealots," that we may be ruffled by the notion of the Lord as a zealot. Let us note, in passing, that zealotry, zealousness, is a prophetic characteristic of a Lord who, confronted by our darkness, rods, boots, blood, and fire, decides to take matters in hand and do something for us we obviously could not do for ourselves, namely, to establish peace, justice, and righteousness.

A baby is coming, bringing a new world order of "justice . . . with righteousness" (9:7). Should we rejoice (9:3) or tremble in our boots?

SECOND LESSON: TITUS 2:11-14

The Epistle announces that "the grace of God has appeared." The announcement is a call to rejoice, to sing, to dance. And so we shall sing tonight, singing as we have never sung before.

The eschatology embodied here asserts, however, that because of the advent of Christ, the time is up for us. A new kingdom requires new citizens. To live by the mores and customs of the old kingdom would be to appear appallingly out of step with the times. Thus the text moves from joyous acclamation to ethical exhortation.

Ethical exhortation may not be what people have in mind when they come to church on Christmas. In fact, this may be the one night when folk hope they can come to church without getting beaten over the head concerning their bad behavior. But there is no side-stepping this call to "live lives that are self-controlled, upright, and godly" (2:12). Someone is here dying to do ethics, even on Christmas.

Titus 2:11-14 is the theological indicative (you *are*) to the preceding list of ethical imperatives (you *should*). "For the grace of God has appeared, bringing salvation to all" (2:11) is the indicative affirmation of faith that is meant as the source for the ethical injunctions found throughout Titus 2. All this ethical advice for old women, slaves, young women, husbands, younger men, and children is founded upon a christological, eschatological affirmation—"the grace of God has appeared, bringing salvation to all."

The preacher may choose to work with the Epistle as a helpful Christmas corrective to any unfounded, detached, vague, yuletide joy. We have not gathered this day merely to "celebrate." We have gathered to ponder the implications of the invasion of God among us. "He it is who gave himself for us that he might redeem us from all iniquity and purify for himself a people of his own who are zealous for good deeds" (Titus 2:14).

An idea for a sermon on the Epistle: "The Ethical Implications of Christmas Carols."

GOSPEL: LUKE 2:1-20

Christmas is a celebration of the church when the preacher may feel overwhelmed by the occasion. Tradition, music, poetry, and congregational expectation all combine to overwhelm the preacher in seasonal richness. There are those who come to church on Christmas with the vague sense of something being right in the world or in themselves that they would like to celebrate, a warm glow they know not how to name but would like to affirm.

The lectionary texts for this day, and our interpretive approach to them, suggest that the homiletical task for Christmas is to rename our vague hopes as Immanuel, to redescribe our yearning as eschatological hope. "The zeal of the LORD of hosts" (Isa. 9:7) is doing something among us and we are dependent upon the preacher's telling us how that something relates to us and where we live this Christmas.

In a way, the tone for our preaching is set by Luke's treatment of the nativity in our Gospel, Luke 2:1-20. For most of us, Luke's is the only nativity we remember, so adept is Luke at telling a story. Even the story's familiarity among the congregation can be used by the preacher as context for eschatological redescription so that the congregation hears new things in an old story, new things of a new kingdom coming.

Note the political setting of the story. Luke is so wonderfully subtle. Without saying, "Now, I am going to say something political," Luke sets the birth in the days of Augustus, the forced "Peace of Augustus" "while Quirinius was governor of Syria," when everyone, even the poor and the pregnant were forced to be registered (2:1-5). Caesar has no means of keeping track of these Jews without proper government registration.

It was here that a baby was born. We are taught by the morning newspaper, the evening news, to know names like Augustus, Quirinius, important government people who use power, who control the masses, who keep records on the population. But we do not know Mary, have never heard of Joseph.

See? Already, without telling us anything explicit, Luke is busy rearranging our ideas about power, about history, about news. Almost as important as the news is who gets the news. The first to hear that a zealous God is making a move against the empire are *shepherds*. Need more be said? The messengers are among the hosts of the Lord (see Isaiah 9:7 and note the militaristic image of the "LORD of hosts"), angels (Luke 2:8-14).

By echoing Old Testament messianic images (compare Mic. 5:2) of Bethlehem as City of David, the manger (see Isa. 1:3), Luke links this birth with the expectation of Israel. A faithful, expectant, oppressed people is about to be delivered, Abraham's seed is about to bless the world.

How? Through a baby. The Isaiah 9:1-7 collision of images is echoed by Luke 2:1-20. Heavenly legions announce to poor shepherds that God's glory is about to be manifested on earth. Power is about to be shifted from the rulers of this world and their methods of governance to God's Anointed

One and his way. We were surprised in hearing Isaiah's announcement "all the boots of the tramping warriors and all the garments rolled in blood shall be burned as fuel for the fire" followed by "for a child has been born for us, a son given to us" (Isa. 9:5-6). Now we are jolted by a story that begins with important, powerful people like Augustus and Quirinius in Jerusalem and Rome and ends with a bunch of nobodies like Mary, Joseph, and shepherds in Bethlehem all summoned to see a baby.

Most empires are toppled, most new kingdoms are established with drumroll, fire, guns, and might. This new, eternal rule is founded by angels' songs, the wonderment of shepherds, and a baby's cry. What is happening here is political, but it is a peculiar politics indeed.

PROCLAIMING THE TEXTS

There are many things we do not know about Jesus. There are large gaps in our information about him, great disagreement over aspects of his life such as his origins. Circumstances of his birth—location, parentage, the "hidden years" of his childhood—are among those aspects of his life upon which there is disagreement or silence in the various Gospels.

The most historically certain facts of Jesus are the circumstances of his death. Marcus Borg (*Jesus: A New Vision* [San Francisco: Harper & Row, 1987], 179) says, "The most certain fact about the historical Jesus is his execution as a political rebel." "Jesus was executed by the Romans as a would-be 'king of the Jews' " (Sanders, *Jesus and Judaism*, 294). "Jesus was crucified by the Romans, on charges that he was a political insurrectionist" (James Charlesworth, *Jesus Within Judaism*, Anchor Bible [New York: Doubleday, 1988], 90).

Well you may ask, Why mention death, crucifixion on Christmas? In order to set in context the nature of our Christmas joy. Our incarnation joy is messianic, apocalyptic joy. The Roman overlords of Judea were not fools, nor were those who greeted the advent of the babe in Bethlehem as the Christ. They knew: *Something political is happening here, something to do with power, who has power, and to whom power is shifting.*

Rudolph Bultmann, so intent on making Jesus make sense within the reigning intellectual establishment's ways of making sense (such as existentialism), argued that the Nazarene's activity was *misunderstood* "as something political." (See Martin Hengel, *The Charismatic Leader and His Followers,* trans. J. Greig [New York: Crossroad, 1981], 38ff., cf. Sanders, *Jesus and Judaism,* 224–26.) No, they knew. The "kingdom of God" that Jesus preached and that Herod clearly perceived as a threat at Jesus' birth (Matthew 2) was, in the words of John Howard Yoder, "a social order and not a hidden one" (*The Politics of Jesus* [Grand Rapids, Mich.: Wm. B.

Eerdmans, 1972], 108). Jesus' birth occurred in the context of nearly constant Judean political rebellion, was undoubtedly read by many as part of "the simmering mutiny that had gripped Palestine for generations" (Joel Carmichael, "The Story of Jesus and the Jewish War," *Midstream* 25 [1979]: 67).

Those who expected Jesus to raise a violent revolt against Rome were wrong. Those political expectations ended in Rome's brutal defeat of the Jewish people in C.E. 70. As for Jesus, "revolt" ended at Calvary just a few years after it began in Bethlehem. There, Jesus was decisively defeated by the Romans in the only way empires have for dealing with threats to their power: officially sanctioned violence.

Yet viewed in the context of the gospel's peculiar brand of politics, the cross was not the end of Jesus' revolt, but rather its beginning. A great, cosmic struggle, the first skirmish of which was fought in Bethlehem, was decisively ended by God in Jesus' favor at Calvary and by the empty tomb on Easter. The kingdoms of this world went head-to-head with the "King" whose reign began in Bethlehem and the baby won.

We are thus arguing for a hermeneutic that reads the nativity "backwards," as it were, the only way Christians know how to read our history, eschatologically, reading backward from the cross and Easter, back through the actions and words of Jesus, back to his birth. Politics is about power. But you and I have severely atrophied notions of power, so our images must be enlarged through this story of Jesus' birth. The nativity, that mystery which we celebrate this Christmas, means to rearrange our notions of politics, means to provide a preliminary delineation of a strange kingdom that takes form among us beginning in the strangest of ways—with a baby.

In pondering texts dealing with the birth of Jesus, we shall want to ask many of the same questions asked about the origins of any great political leaders: Where were they born? To whom were they born? What do the setting and circumstances of their origins tell us that may be of help in understanding their later significance?

The continuing scandal of Jesus as Messiah was that Jesus appeared to fit so few of the requirements for a messiah. Paul M. van Buren argues that Jesus could not have been Israel's Messiah because so little he accomplished marked him "as the inaugurator of the Messianic age. The Messianic age . . . is marked by radical historical transformation" ("Affirmation of the Jewish People," *Journal of the American Academy of Religion* 45 [1977]: 1090). To put the matter more bluntly, more relevant to the birth of the child at Bethlehem, in the face of the death of Jewish children in the *Shoah*, van Buren asks, "Can any Christian say that Jesus was or is the Messiah?" The scandal of Christian assertion is that we claim that, in this baby at Bethlehem, we really do see the long-awaited, politically disruptive messiah we had been taught by Israel to expect.

All of this serious theology before we begin our homiletics is meant to remind the Christmas preacher that large matters are before the church this night. Luke is pondering many of the same fundamental questions about Jesus that continue to trouble us. Why do so many still look upon Jesus and not see the Messiah? If this baby Jesus really were God's answer to the problems of the world, why was that answer not more self-evident, right at the beginning?

The Nativity of Our Lord, 2
The Service in the Day

Lutheran	Roman Catholic	Episcopal	Common Lectionary
Isa. 52:7-10	Isa. 52:7-10	Isa. 52:7-10	Isa. 52:7-10
Heb. 1:1-9	Heb. 1:1-6	Heb. 1:1-12	Heb. 1:1-12
John 1:1-14	John 1:1-18	John 1:1-14	John 1:1-14

FIRST LESSON: ISAIAH 52:7-10

If your congregation has made the most of Advent, restraining itself through weeks of steadily growing anticipation, limiting its repertoire to Advent hymns and waiting to sing Christmas carols, now is the time to at last pull out all the stops on the organ, dress the altar in festive white, and allow the light of Christmas Day to flow into the church in all its brilliance.

Our first lesson, Isaiah 52:7-10, is meant to be sung rather than said. We need a choir, a full orchestra to do this hymn right. Rather than to analyze this passage, pick it apart, subject it to critical scrutiny like a cadaver on a slab, your time would be better spent in attempting to secure for your service this day the Mormon Tabernacle Choir. Failing at that, at least keep the poetry as poetry, the songs as song if you must preach today.

The whole city has been waiting in edgy expectation. Some have said that the king is coming, but who knows when? Walter Brueggemann reminds us that these "promises are addressed only to people in exile who have seen the city fall (40:2) and have suffered the loss of their entire world. . . . The promises are not available to us while we are people who cling to the old city and to old organizations of reality" ("Second Isaiah" in Seitz, *Reading and Preaching Isaiah*, 71). Some people, too often disappointed by false hope, cynically go about their business, certain that no royal parade will march through town today. Others, more stubborn in their refusal to give up messianic expectation, scan the horizon for any sign of advent.

As we noted in our commentary on the Gospel for the First Sunday in Advent (Mark 13:33-37), for most of our history, God appears to have been absent. Catalog all of the prophets' cries to God to "tear open the heavens and come down" (Isa. 64:1), Jesus' many parables of absentee landlords, vacationing masters, and late bridegrooms, and you have a great deal of absence. We have many more texts that tell us what to do when God does not answer, is not here, does not hear, fails to intervene, refuses to act than we have texts that tell us how to throw a suitable welcome home party for God.

So forgive us—now that Christmas has at last come, the nativity is now, and advent expectation is real presence—for not knowing exactly what to do or say. We are better at waiting than at welcome. Isaiah suggests that today is less a time to do or to say and more a time to sing, "Your God reigns" (Isa. 52:7).

Earlier, on the Second Sunday in Advent (Isa. 40:1-11), the voice of God promised homecoming for exiles. Now, on Christmas, the voices of former exiles are lifted in praise for the homecoming of God, "the return of the LORD to Zion" (Isa. 52:8). The Lord, who appears to have deserted Israel, left Israel to its own devices, is at last returning to God's chosen human family. Now, everybody on earth, even those outside the bounds of God's family, even nations who do not know the story of promised deliverance and restoration, "shall see the salvation of our God" (Isa. 52:10).

Only praise poetry will do to speak of this divine homecoming, only radiant exultation. Poetic metaphor is heaped on metaphor. "How beautiful upon the mountains are the feet of the messenger who announces peace, who brings good news, who announces salvation, . . ." (52:7). On this glad day of days, even dusty feet look beautiful because they bear such good news. Even feet.

In response to the message, the city stirs to its feet, the sentinels begin to shout and sing (52:8), even the rubble and ruin of Jerusalem break forth into song (52:9). Everything that breathes has now grabbed a tambourine or trumpet, or is standing on tops of the pews, singing for all they are worth. With even rubble and ruin making music, who needs the Mormon Tabernacle Choir? Today, God's homecoming, everybody, everything (cf. Psalm 150) becomes a musician.

Here the church has reached back into its collective memory to recall what may have been a song for the triumphant arrival of a victorious king (see James Luther Mays, "Isaiah's Royal Theology and the Messiah" in Seitz, *Reading and Preaching the Book of Isaiah*, 39–51). The good news is news of a royal victory, now transposed into a higher key to praise the triumphant victory of the God who "has bared his holy arm before the eyes of all the nations (52:10; cf. Deut. 26:8). But let us be clear that this joyous parade is no Fourth of July victory parade for the heroes of Desert Storm—look how *we* have triumphed and killed and conquered. This parade is for the homecoming of God. Earlier, on the First Sunday in Advent, Jesus suggested that the master's midnight return was a threatening possibility for sleeping servants (Mark 13:33-37). Yet we find, on

Christmas Day, that the God whose arrival we feared is now joyously welcomed as our Savior.

One hopes that our Advent sermons have been honest, for, as Brueggemann says, "To use the poetry of homecoming without prior literature of *exile* is cheap grace" ("Second Isaiah," in Seitz, *Reading and Preaching Isaiah*, 71). Joy does not arise from collective ecclesiastical relief that Christmas is only a "spiritual" or "religious" event. Use of words like "King" and "reign" are meant to make explicit economic, political claims about the demise of the present government in order to make way for new rule. If we have learned well enough, during the reflective, somber days of Advent, to let go of the present order, its false gods and deceitful securities, we may be better able to be embraced by the good news that "Your God reigns."

Homecoming in Isaiah is reiterated in the incarnational poetry of John's prologue: "And the Word became flesh and lived among us, and we have seen his glory, the glory as of a father's only son, full of grace and truth" (John 1:14).

Commentators note that these "tidings" are not the event of homecoming, but rather the proclamation of the event. Isaiah has rendered for us that moment when we receive the news, that instant when we hear the messenger's message, "Your God reigns." This is much like the moment when you heard from the surgeon that the operation was a success, she would live; when you finally got the call through after the storm and heard the voice on the other end say, "Mom, I'm OK." Ponder these moments, recall how you immediately burst into song on the way back to the kitchen after getting the good news. Nobody walks away from such news without a song.

SECOND LESSON: HEBREWS 1:1-9

The similarities between today's Epistle from the letter to the Hebrews and today's Gospel, the prologue to John, are too similar to be merely coincidental. Let us read the first verses of Hebrews as poetic prologue to John's even more wonderfully poetic prologue.

Speaking is primary here, the speech of watchmen on the city walls, the speech of a ruined city's rubble (Isa. 52:7-10), the speech of the incarnate Logos (John 1:1-14), the speech of the prophets of old and now "in these last days he has spoken to us by a Son" (Heb. 1:2). Ours is a loquacious God, a God determined to have conversation with creation. As the author of Hebrews notes, this talkative God has spoken to us "in many and various ways" (Heb. 1:1). Now, in the most dramatic and incarnate of communicative events, "he has spoken to us by a Son." Jesus is the supreme event of God's loving self-communication.

Hebrews shares John's notion of the preexistence of Christ ("In the beginning was the Word. . . . All things came into being through him. . . ," John 1:1-3). The Christ is also the "heir," the creator of "all worlds," "reflection of God's glory," the "exact imprint of God's very being." Forget your Lukan images of the vulnerable babe in the straw of a manger. Hebrews pushes a high Christology in which the incarnate one holds all of creation in the palm of his hand.

So "in the beginning" (Gen. 1:1) when creation was being formed from chaos, the Son was "in the beginning" (John 1:1). Nothing that is, is so without the Son's bidding. "Sweet Little Jesus Boy" is a fine hymn but Hebrews would rather sing "Of the Father's Love Begotten."

Not only was this Son, this present Word at the beginning, Hebrews says he also rules now and forever "at the right hand of the majesty on high" (Heb. 1:3), a good deal higher than angels. Apparently, presumptuous angels were a big problem for the church of the letter to the Hebrews. The author expends the next six verses (1:4-9) amassing quotes from the royal Psalms of enthronement (Pss. 2:7; 45:6-7), ascribing their accolades to Jesus, putting angels in their place, a place considerably lower than the exalted Son.

Our problem is not angels who are too big but rather a God who is too small. Anemic, modern Christologies that render a congenial, empathetic but essentially impotent Christ are too timid for these first verses of Hebrews, this magnificent hymn to the superiority of Christ. Do we yet have the language to praise such a Christ? Is it possible for us, having been so determinedly realistic about the brokenness and the fallenness of this waiting world, to be as incarnationally realistic about our redemption? Will we stand this bright day, face-to-face with the world, and dare to sing of what we have seen, to testify to what we now know, even in the midst of our lack of redemption?

> The LORD has bared his holy arm
>   before the eyes of all the nations;
> and all the ends of the earth shall see
>   the salvation of our God."
>   (Isaiah 52:10)

GOSPEL: JOHN 1:1-18

Today's third Christmas hymn is more familiar to us. We love to hear John's prologue, though we may not be too sure of its meaning. Like most good music, John 1 is experienced before it is understood.

"Yea, Lord, we greet thee, born this happy morning," is an appropriate summary of this prologue. We are surely encountering a hymn here. Verses

1:1-5, 10-12, 14, 16 almost throb with rhythmic poetry. In a delightful mix of adopted Hellenistic philosophical terms with Hebrew concepts, the hymn begins John's Gospel with pure praise for the incarnation.

It is well that today's service is held during the day, for this is a text of light. Evoking memories of that light-evoking creative Spirit that hovered over the dark pre-creation chaos (Genesis 1), that divine Word that brought forth light, John links the "light" that now dawns in a previously darkened world. That light has evoked "children of God" (1:12), a new people, a new family (church), as if out of nothing. So the people who sing this Logos hymn are also the living, breathing evidence of its truth. A light really has shone in the darkness. As if from out of nothing, God got children (1:12)—us.

The people who sing this hymn are those blinded by the light of God in Jesus, having experienced the fullness of God. Even though "no one has ever seen God," this only Son, the one who was God and was with God at the beginning, the "light," this one "has made him known" (John 1:18).

PROCLAIMING THE TEXTS

Isaiah 52 is a song of homecoming. God is coming home to Israel. The people who once knew no songs but funeral dirges together "sing for joy" at "the return of the LORD to Zion" (Isa. 52:3). A further reading of Isaiah 52:11-12 shows that this is also a homecoming for the exiles. The prophet bids exiles to gather their belongings, especially the sacred "vessels of the LORD" (52:11) and return home with Yahweh both as leader and rear guard (52:12).

These verses may have special significance for you as you look out upon your Christmas congregation and see old, familiar faces now home for the holidays. Christmas also has a way of calling back a few of your long-lost "exiles" back to church. Something about Christmas, perhaps something even deeper than the superficial yuletide sentiment, draws some folk back toward the church at this time of year. Isaiah bids us to see this Christmas, for God and for ourselves, as homecoming. Pray that God might use this service and your words to welcome exiles back home.

Isn't it interesting that many of us have Christmas Eve services, but no service on Christmas Day? Why are the crowds better at my church on Christmas Eve than on the day itself? Christmas Day trips away to friends and relatives may be one reason, but one suspects it is not the real reason. It is as if we all do better living with anticipation than experiencing reality. We become accustomed to not having, adapted to bereavement, as if mourning were normal. John says of Jesus, "He came to his own, and his

45

own people did not accept him" (1:11). Behind this Johannine polemic against fellow Jews in the synagogue lies a hint of our Christmas Day problem—we all become so adjusted to the darkness that we become blinded by true light.

All of today's texts make some extravagant claims for God. Isaiah's God, who "has bared his holy arm" (52:10), becomes Hebrews' cosmic Son who "sustains all things by his powerful word" (1:3), and is John's eternal Word by whom "the world came into being" (1:10). If early Christians had any reservations about making large claims for Christ, such christological modesty is thrown to the wind in today's texts. Every divine claim, every godly accolade that could be applied to God is now, in the prologues to Hebrews and John, heaped upon Jesus. Nothing is created by the Father that is not also from the hands of the Son (John 1:3, 10; Heb. 1:2). Even the light of the sun is the light of the Son (John 1:4-5, 9). No angel on high is higher than he (Heb. 1:4-9). Here is no Christology for the doctrinally faint of heart or the theologically timid.

If we have done our homiletical work well in the past Sundays of Advent, our congregations may be ready to embrace this shining, cosmic Christ. If we have been honest about the absence of God, the pain of this fallen, darkened world, our people may be ready for the homecoming of a Redeemer who is large, preexistent, eternal, who knows how to reign. If you are blessed with a congregation who happens to be economically deprived, socially marginalized, culturally disenfranchised, any less of a Christ than the one rendered by the poetic prologues of Hebrews and John is too little a Christ to help, too little an event to induce us to sing.

Here comes a large, blindingly bright Son whose homecoming parade causes even our city's urban ruins to sing (Isa. 52:9). For so much of the church's year, we are far too timid about our claims, far too respectful and deferential of the regnant principalities and powers, much too at home in the darkness. But not today. Today, Christmas, stirred to recognition by poets named Isaiah, Hebrews, and John, even the most numbed, dumb among us sing, "for in plain sight they see the return of the LORD to Zion" (Isa. 52:8).

Admittedly, such pushy, extravagant Christology is not in vogue these days. Jesus is rendered, by contemporary theology, into the merely empathetic, and essentially impotent, friend. We may believe that on Christmas this scaled-down God came to stand beside us, but we stammer in attempting to describe what this God now can do for us. Part of the problem may be one of social location. If we happen to be living in a neighborhood without rubble (Isa. 52:9), we may not understand those who spontaneously pour into the streets and break into victory chants at the news, the Gospel, "Your God reigns" (Isa. 52:7).

In my last parish I led a group in reading Harold Kushner's popular book *When Bad Things Happen to Good People*. Most of the group liked the book, finding Kushner's image of a caring, sensitive, empathetic God similar to our own. For most of us, that was God enough.

But not for Tom. "Why would anybody pray to this God?" Tom asked after reading Kushner's chapter on the book of Job. "For that matter, why would anybody shake his fist, cry out for answers from, fall down and worship this God? This God's too tame, too damn caring, and too little active to be the God of the Bible."

At first I thought Tom was being too harsh. Then I remembered. Tom is a recovering alcoholic. The bondage in his life was considerably more formidable than ours, impervious to the petty assaults of mild self-help therapy. In his AA group, Tom had been taught to admit, "We were powerless over our own lives" then, "We had to reach out to a power greater than ourselves."

Pray that you will have the opportunity to preach to someone like Tom this Christmas. When he hears the exuberant claims of Isaiah 52, Hebrews 1, or John's hymn, he will know how to sing.

For many Sundays we have been praying, "Thy kingdom come." Today, says Isaiah, we are about to have our prayers answered: "Your God reigns."

First Sunday after Christmas

Lutheran	Roman Catholic	Episcopal	Common Lectionary
Isa. 45:22-25	Gen. 15:1-6; 21:1-3	Isa. 61:10—62:3	Isa. 61:10—62:3
Col. 3:12-17	Heb. 11:8, 11-12, 17-19	Gal. 3:23-25; 4:4-7	Gal. 4:4-7
Luke 2:25-40	Luke 2:22-40	John 1:1-18	Luke 2:22-40

FIRST LESSON: ISAIAH 61:10—62:3

Both the Common Lectionary and the Episcopal Lectionary use portions of Isaiah 61–62 (read in part on the Third Sunday in Advent). Used this Sunday, it is meant to continue the extravagant rejoicing that occupied the church on Christmas Day as well as to provide a prelude to the joyful song of Simeon and the testimony of Anna (Luke 2:25-40). The Lutherans use Isaiah 45:22-25 this Sunday, a poem on the spread of the word to the ends of the earth, a poem that provides an appropriate prelude to Simeon's song. The Roman Lectionary, determined by that church's designation of this as the Feast of the Holy Family, goes its own way with the institution of Abraham and Sarah's family in Genesis 15 and 21.

Our cue comes from Isaiah 61:10, "I will greatly rejoice in the LORD." Yahweh has thrown a fancy dress ball and provided the clothing for free— garments of salvation and robes of righteousness. The raucous sounds of this global praise party extend to every nation on earth (61:11).

Knowing what is to come in today's Gospel (Luke 2:25-40) attracts us to the opening verse of chapter 62, "For Zion's sake I will not keep silent, and for Jerusalem's sake I will not rest." "I will not rest" is perhaps better translated, "I will not restrain myself." Someone has begun to sing here, and matters of propriety, sober restraint, and caution pale before the realization of "salvation like a burning torch" (62:1).

Appropriately eschatological, political questions are: Who would be threatened by the Christmas songs of poor people? Why should the authorities be made uneasy by Christmas parties in the ghetto? What harm could possibly come from a few slaves singing Gospel songs about salvation? Perhaps the police have taken our chants about "a burning torch" too literally. What harm can Christmas poetry do to the reigning powers?

If you know the answers to these questions, you may be well on your way to understanding why Isaiah was Jesus' favorite poet.

SECOND LESSON: GALATIANS 4:4-7

"But when the fullness of time had come" (Gal.4:4). There is much fullness in today's texts. Once again, one wonders if we modern preachers are better at naming signs of emptiness in the world than in proclaiming fullness. Today's Epistle reminds us that the fullness which we continue to celebrate today is not some vague, universal culmination of general human aspiration. This is fullness *of* time, *in* time, Jesus. He was not some external ideal that floated down from ethereal realms. He was "born of a woman." He was "born under the law," a faithful, obedient child of Israel and its Torah (as today's Gospel, Luke 2:25-40 demonstrates).

Such historical particularity and specificity may be a helpful homiletical corrective against possible sermonic slippage into vague sentiment and mushy platitudes in sermons at this time of year. The incarnation in "the fullness of time" is considerably more significant than helium-filled balloons named "peace," "goodwill," and "joy" that float over the congregation, untied from the historical particularities of where we actually live. He, Jesus, came among us, folk who live in Durham and Des Moines, bound to rules and ideals we rarely obey, making us children who now address the once distant, omnipotent, omniscient God as "Abba!" "Daddy" (Gal. 4:4-7).

Is Paul here affirming Jesus' virgin birth (Gal. 4:4), as both Matthew and Luke attest but elsewhere Paul seems to know nothing about? Probably Paul's "born of a woman" is his way of reiterating the full, utter humanity of Jesus. A beloved Pauline theme (see Phil. 2:5-11, Rom. 1:3; 7:4; 9:5; 2 Cor. 8:9), the humanity of Christ might provide a fruitful point of emphasis for the preacher in these days of celebration of the incarnation. Note that Paul sees the humanity of Christ as integrally related to our "adoption as children" (4:5). If the preacher followed the suggestion to focus upon the power and majesty of Christ (The Nativity of Our Lord, 2), then this Sunday's sermon might strike a counter christological note— the humanity of Christ. Here in Galatians 3:23-25, 4:4-7, Paul depicts the incarnation as God's means of lifting up our status from that of those who are "imprisoned and guarded under the law" (3:23) to those who now are on such familial, close terms with God as "children" and "heirs" (4:7) that we now call God "Daddy." While one may not want to push the familial analogy too far, it is true that the relationship between masters and slaves is of a considerably different order than that of parents and children. That which the law once did through discipline and imprisonment (3:23), the Spirit now performs "in our hearts" (4:6). The everyday, concrete, ethical implications of this new, post-incarnation, filial relationship might be made explicit in the sermon. Because we could not come up to

God, in an amazing act of "loving condescension" (Barth), God came down to us. Divine downward mobility (Phil. 2:5-11) makes all the difference.

Take care in making too sharp a distinction between pre-Christmas life "imprisoned and guarded under the law" (3:23) and post-Christmas life "justified by faith." Recent Pauline scholarship suggests that most of our old "law–gospel" dichotomy is more the result of reformation polemic than Pauline thought (see Gerald S. Sloyan, *Is Christ the End of the Law?* [Philadelphia: Westminster, 1978]). Paul's problem with Torah was not that it was too legalistic, conservative, or narrow but that it was not Christ. The advent of the Son shifts our relationship to God in a way that relativizes Torah rather than negates it.

In fact, Paul seems to stress that the Son was a child of Israel, "born under the law" (4:4). Linked with today's Gospel, the post-nativity narrative of Luke 2:22-40, today's Epistle can be an invitation to the preacher to stress the "Jewishness" of Jesus rather than to raise questions about his parentage through the false opposition of law with gospel. Luke 2:39 portrays Jesus' parents as scrupulous adherents to the Mosaic law. Whatever this "fullness of time" means for Paul and the Galatians, it means in great part the fulfillment of the hopes of *Israel*, not their negation.

As Paul M. van Buren says,

> "And the Word happened as [or became, was made] flesh" (John 1:14). It was of course Jewish flesh, for the only God whom the church knows is just this God who has chosen to work by means of this particular people for the good of the whole. "Incarnation" cannot say less than this. The church cannot properly say "incarnation" without saying "Jew" at the same moment. It has no Lord but the Jew Jesus, and Jesus had no calling from and made no response to any but the God of the Jewish people. If the incarnation comes from the heart of this God, then it points to the heart of the Covenant and so, in pointing to Israel's God, it points also to God's Israel (*A Theology of Jewish–Christian Reality* [San Francisco: Harper & Row, 1988], xvii-xix).

This provides a nice homiletical transition to today's Gospel.

GOSPEL: LUKE 2:22-40

(For John 1:1-18, see The Nativity of Our Lord, 2, The Service in the Day.)

When we left Luke's narrative of the nativity on Christmas Eve (Luke 2:1-20) everyone was singing. Gabriel sang (Luke 1:26-35, the Fourth Sunday in Advent), Zechariah sang (Luke 1:68-79), the angels sang (Luke 2:13-14), and now old Simeon sings (2:28-32). Obviously, Isaiah's cue, "rejoice in the Lord" (Isa. 61:10) has set a chain-reaction chorus on heaven and on earth. The significance of these Christmas carols is not only in *what* is being sung but also in *who* is doing the singing.

The Gospel begins, not with singing, but with religious duties. The angels' songs and midnight visits from the shepherds were fine, but now life appears to be moving back to normal. Mary and Joseph have brought their baby up to the temple to present him to the Lord "as it is written in the law of the Lord" (2:23). Everything is done by the book—Torah, that is—supported by quotes from Exodus 13:1-2 and Leviticus 12:6. All of this is in keeping with Luke's intention to demonstrate that Jesus' parents and Jesus himself are good, obedient, devout Jews. Many strange, wonderful things have happened in Luke in the last few days, but Luke seems intent on arguing that essentially nothing utterly *new* has occurred. What may seem new, weird, odd is really, to Torah-knowledgeable people, the fulfillment of the hopes of and the promises made to Israel. Everything is done in accordance with the Torah, including the offer of "a pair of turtledoves or two young pigeons" (2:24).

The rather marginal mention of these turtledoves and pigeons is so typical of Luke's method of preaching. By referring to these little birds, almost incidentally, Luke reveals something about this Mary and Joseph and their baby—they are poor. Turtledoves and pigeons are a suitable dedicatory offering for the purification of a mother of a male child, but only if the parents are poor. A lamb is the prescribed offering for the mother, yet "if she cannot offer a lamb, then she shall take two turtledoves and two young pigeons" (Lev. 12:6-8).

These birds of the poor lead us to the testimony of old Simeon. While at the temple, Joseph and Mary encounter a man who "was righteous and devout, looking forward to the consolation of Israel" (2:25). Frame the scene in your mind. Against the backdrop of the magnificent temple, moving among the masses, we encounter a poor couple from the hinterland, an old man waiting to die, and (2:36-38) an old, visionary woman. The story has deliberately turned our gaze away from the people and places of power. No priests or officials have appeared in the nativity story. All we have are a few shepherds, a poor peasant couple, and a couple of old people with little better to do with the time on their hands than to hang out down at the temple. It is among these people—the poor, the old, and the very young and weak—that the "glory to your people Israel" (2:32) is appearing. The voiceless—the poor, the very old, the very young—are singing. "For Zion's sake I will not keep silent" (Isa. 62:1).

Taking the child in his wrinkled hands, Simeon praised God (2:28-32). Eyes, old, dimmed eyes "have seen your salvation" (2:30), "a light for revelation to the Gentiles" (2:32). "Vindication shines like the dawn, and her salvation like a burning torch" (Isa. 62:1).

Yet not all is light in Simeon's song. Simeon blesses the "amazed" (2:33) peasant couple. The "blessing" is an odd one indeed. Mary is warned that her baby "is destined for the falling and rising of many in Israel," he is "a sign that will be opposed" (2:34). The temple is not only a scene of blessing and praise, it is also a place of death. The priest slits the throats of the squawking turtledoves. Jesus is the stone that temple builders rejected (Luke 20:17-18). If Simeon has seen, here, in cuddly flesh, "the consolation of Israel" (2:25), consolation will not come cheap. Mary's advent song had prophesied her baby's arrival as a time of dislocation, of class struggle, the casting down of the proud and the liftup of the lowly (Luke 1:46-55). Simeon's song confirms her dark presentiments. "A sword will pierce your own soul too" (2:35). Some bloody "blessing" is this.

Old, half-crazed Anna is given the last word. Her ancestor is Hannah (1 Sam. 2:1-10). She is old, a widow, therefore poor (Luke 2:36). Now, at eighty-four, "she never left the temple but worshiped there with fasting and prayer night and day" (2:37). In other words, she is a "bag lady," who, if it were not for the sheltering portico of the temple, would perish in the cold. I once met her and a couple of her sisters of the streets in a little Lutheran church in Philadelphia. The church with the open door is their only home. With no one to go home to, no home to go home to, of course she spends a lot of time at the church; she's got nowhere else better to go. Her suffering is not in the abstract, but in the utterly, undeniably concrete. Old, poor, alone, she has brought her suffering to church, to the temple, to be sanctified. Upon seeing the child, Anna breaks into praise, telling anybody who would listen that here was the "redemption of Jerusalem" (2:38).

Old people and a newborn baby, a befuddled peasant couple and a couple of visionary old people, enlightening eyes that see, even in the dark gloom of the temple, exuberant blessing and blood sacrifice, recognition by the poor and resistance by Mary, Israel consoled and a sword thrust deep into the soul. What is being born among us?

That surely is the question we are meant to ask as we return to Galilee, back to post-holiday responsibilities, with a blessed and amazed Mary, Joseph, and Jesus. What is being born among us?

Behind the manger, after the songs of angels, and the righteous completion of "everything required by the law" (2:39), Simeon sees the stark, foreboding image of a cross.

PROCLAIMING THE TEXTS

The old church calendar, in its wisdom, places immediately after the joyful feast of the Nativity, the day of St. Stephen (December 26), first martyr of the church in Acts; and the day of the Holy Innocents, victims of the bloody Bethlehem massacre according to Matthew 2:13-18 (December 28). New birth and nativity, the cross and sacrifice appear to go together in the Gospel. Nothing truly new, no large move of God occurs without some pain. Blood and birth go together.

We began this Sunday's encounter with the texts with an invitation from Isaiah 61:10, "I will rejoice in the LORD." The white upon the altar proclaims Christmas and its Sundays as a season of extravagant, unrestrained joy, a fitting response to this the "fullness of time" (Gal. 4:4). Then the Gospel (Luke 2:25-40) introduces us to two old people who have been waiting a long time for time's fullness, Simeon and Anna. These two marginalized, fringe characters, "little people" who emerge from out of nowhere, have their say, then recede again into the darkness, apparently the only people up at the temple who know what is going on. To them is given the eyes to see and voices to say what God is doing in the world in this little baby. So much for the biblical scholars, priests, theologians, and government planners, Luke seems to say. If you want to know what's really going on, ask the people on the bottom or out on the fringe. We who live in a society that has ways of marginalizing our very old and our very young ought to sit up and take note.

Simeon's words expand our notions of "blessings." Whatever "salvation" (Luke 2:30) is at work for Israel here, whatever joy exudes from our worship this Sunday, it is no simple joy, no cheap salvation. Simeon's talk of falling and rising, of opposition and piercing swords (2:34-35) invites homiletical reflection upon the depth and complexity of God's ways among us. Simeon offers a helpful corrective against the yuletide tendency to float off into superficial sentimentality, to reduce our testimony to a Christmas card slogan or our salvation songs to advertising jingles. The nativity, as Simeon says, is about social dislocation, about confused parents, and dark forebodings. Caesar has an answer for old Jews who get too uppity with their singing—his answer is a sword. On the hill beyond the Bethlehem manger, there is a cross awaiting a suitable victim.

Now that the yuletide commercial buying and selling and getting and giving is at last spent, now that the surrounding world has at last tired of Christmas and is gearing up for New Year's Eve parties, the church is left to ponder the true significance of what has been born among us. Soberly, reflectively, we gather to be instructed by Isaiah, Simeon, Anna, and Paul on the nature of our salvation.

The Name of Jesus
(January 1)

Lutheran	Roman Catholic	Episcopal	Common Lectionary
Num. 6:22-27	Num. 6:22-27	Exod. 34:1-8	Num. 6:22-27
Rom. 1:1-7 or Phil. 2:9-13	Gal. 4:4-7	Rom. 1:1-7	Gal. 4:4-7 or Phil. 2:9-13
Luke 2:21	Luke 2:16-21	Luke 2:15-21	Luke 2:15-21

FIRST LESSON: NUMBERS 6:22-27

One of the forgotten gestures within the church's repertoire is blessing. "The LORD bless you and keep you" (Num. 6:24) connects us with the primal activity of imparting power from one person to another through blessing. Through blessing (*berekah* in Hebrew), we construct the conditions whereby *shalom* is possible. When cultic gatherings end, there is a blessing, a benediction. That is what priests do in Israel, they bless people in the tradition of "Aaron and his sons" (Num. 6:23).

The Gospels depict Jesus as God's blessing (Gal. 3:8-9). Jesus shocks his contemporaries by blessing children (Mark 10:13-16). He blesses meals (Mark 6:41; 8:6-7; and parallels). He blesses his disciples (Luke 24:50-51). Jesus shows the radically different nature of his kingdom by having his people even bless those who curse them (Luke 6:28). They are thereby living witnesses to the God who manages to bless by rain and sun even the "just" and the "unjust" (Matt. 5:45). Poorly done, half-hearted, limited benedictions and blessings, in worship or in daily life, are an affront to the effusive, gracious God of blessing.

We have long ago secularized our times of leave-taking, but the words we use, even in ordinary, daily speech, hearken back to the theological significance of blessing as committing another to the sustaining care of God. The French *adieu,* the Spanish *adios,* the English "good-bye" are all linguistically derived from "God be with you."

In this priestly blessing in Numbers, the priest blesses the people by imparting to them the "face of the LORD" (Num. 6:25-26). When a monarch lifts his face to you, he is looking with favor upon you, noticing you, blessing you with royal recognition.

Blessing someone is literally "putting God's name on them" (Num. 6:27). Names, particularly God's name, have power. Our names are the most intimate, most particular, linguistically evocative aspects of us. If you know a person's name, you know the person. Just speaking the name evokes the person's presence. Thus, to pray "in Jesus' name" is to pray like Jesus, with Jesus.

Note that in the church, unlike in the Old Testament priesthood, there is no special class of priestly elites who possess the power to bless. In this new priestly community, everyone may pray "in the name of Jesus," all have the ability, even the obligation (see Matthew 10, Luke 10) to bless others whom they encounter.

In the light of Numbers 6:22-27, we may justifiably think of Christians as those who go forth into the world performing the priestly work of laying the name of Jesus on people, blessing people by bearing in our lives the face, the countenance of Christ. (See my "Blessing: The Sustaining Presence," in *The Bible: A Sustaining Presence in the Church* [Valley Forge, Pa.: Judson Press, 1981], 97–105.)

Contemporary theologies of liberation speak of God's occasional intervention on behalf of the oppressed. For some time we have envisioned a God who acts, who periodically intrudes into history doing mighty acts. Blessing is a visible, corporeal enactment of another aspect of divine love— providence. Even as God graciously upholds us with blessings as unspectacular as sun and rain, so God is as near to us as the comforting hand of a friend on our shoulder, the loving touch, food, wine, a warm face.

When Christians part from one another at the end of the service of worship on Sunday, when we leave the hospital room of a sister or brother who is ill, when we send a beloved child back to school after the Christmas holidays, these are all occasions for blessing, for the entrusting of another person to the care and daily providence of God. Christians are none other than those who bless in the name of Jesus, in the manner of Jesus.

SECOND LESSON: ROMANS 1:1-7
(OR PHILIPPIANS 2:9-13)

The Lutherans and Episcopalians use Paul's salutation in Romans as a way of pondering the significance of the name of Jesus. Other churches read the great Christ-hymn in Philippians 2:9-13, where all knees bend at the name of Jesus, "the name that is above every name." (Catholics continue Christmas reflection upon Mary's significance through their reading of Galatians 4:4-7, "born of woman.")

The Romans salutation is a marvelous vignette of Paul's Gospel, a sweeping review from the prophets, through David, in the Spirit, by the resurrection (Rom. 1:2-4). While earlier Advent and Christmas readings have clearly depicted Jesus as the fulfillment of the hopes of God to Israel, here is our first mention during this season of Jesus as hope also for the Gentiles (1:5). In the name of Jesus, the gospel is beginning to embrace a wide array of persons. "In the name of . . ." is a royal tag, the words someone uses when that person, as an emissary of a monarch, invokes the king's or queen's name as authority for some act. Our Old Testament lesson suggested the priestly emphasis of blessing, "In the name of. . . ." Now we see that the Epistle lends itself to the royal connotation of invoking the authority of the monarch in claiming territory for king. The territory being claimed here is the Gentiles.

The very presence of your congregation this day is testimony to the weird array of nations that have been gathered "for the sake of his name" (1:5). That name, since Paul, has been laid upon every nation, every people, forming church *ex nihilo*, without the conventional means of human gathering—means like race, gender, social class—with nothing more to convene us than we "are called to belong to Jesus Christ" (1:6). If any doubt the power of that name, all they need do is look at the church, that gathering from among all the nations "for the sake of his name." The babe at Bethlehem is now busy gathering all peoples into a great, global kingdom through baptism.

I regret that my church, the United Methodist, has no tradition of gathering to worship on this day of the Name of Jesus. We have a historic Covenant Service on New Year's Eve bequeathed to us by the Wesleyan tradition, but no tradition for worship at the Name of Jesus. This is unfortunate because the Name of Jesus, January 1, is a marvelous occasion to ponder the power of that name, the way it blesses us, names us, gathers us. This day is a wonderful time to re-vision ourselves as those who are chosen to bear that name before the world, "including yourselves who are called to belong to Jesus Christ" (Rom. 1:6).

GOSPEL: LUKE 2:21

A little one-verse snippet on naming is the whole of the Gospel on this day. But how much is contained in that name! The "eight days" that are mentioned here are the requisite days before circumcision (Lev. 12:3) and naming (Luke 1:59). Matthew appears to make much more of the etymology of Jesus' name in his account of the dream of Joseph (Matt. 1:21). One might have expected Luke to refer us to "Jesus" as the Greek equivalent of Joshua, the name of the leader of God's people into the promised land.

Instead, Luke reminds us that this name was given straight from the mouth of the angel (1:19, 26). When she heard of all this, back at the beginning of this strange nativity story, Mary had said to the angel "let it be with me according to your word" (1:38), which is considerably more than we might have said, considering the strange words that the angel had spoken.

But now we see, at the end of this peculiar story, that everything the angel had promised has happened just as it was spoken. Mary had no idea, in the beginning, what all this meant. Yet she was willing to wait, to trust the angel's word, to be a "servant of the Lord" (Luke 1:38). Earlier, we might have been content to receive our information from historians, or statisticians, or public opinion pollsters. With an intrusive, active God, history, what "9 out of 10 Americans believe," our present experience, what happened the day before yesterday, are all of limited help in predicting what may happen today. We must therefore be prepared to get our facts from angels. The naming of Jesus in Luke is thus a possible ending for the first act of the drama of the incarnation. Mary's trust in the word of the Lord, the message from the angel, has been vindicated. Having seen how everything has happened as the angel has foretold it, we know now that we had better pay close attention to the messages of angels.

PROCLAIMING THE TEXTS

Neither Mary nor Joseph shall name this child. This child is from God and part of the eternal purposes of God (cf. Rom. 1:2-3). Here, toward the end of our celebration of Christmas, we are given an opportunity to reflect with the visiting shepherds upon what "they had heard and seen, as it had been told them" (Luke 2:20), to join Mary who "treasured all these words and pondered them in her heart" (Luke 2:19).

What's in a name? When I hear the name Martin Luther King, Jr., I think of a hot afternoon by the reflecting pool in Washington, D.C., surrounded by thousands, hearing those stirring words of a great preacher leading us to freedom. All you need do is to speak the name and my mind, my memory, my heart will do the rest. In a name is a person, a personality, a history, a world. The pronouncing of the name is not merely a shorthand way of calling memories of that person's presence to mind, it is to make that person present, here, in the most explicit and intimate of ways.

Jesus.

To say, "I am doing this in the name of the people of North Carolina," is to give my actions wider significance, to name under what authority I am here, toward what goal I am moving. To say, "Bless you in the name of Jesus," is to give my action deeper, wider significance. It is to link our present to a holy past, to soar beyond this place and claim what we do with one another to have cosmic, eternal significance. We are here, not under our own compulsion, not merely for ends that we can name; we are here "in the name of Jesus."

Israel is a people "called by the name of the LORD" (Deut. 28:10). Messengers of God are simply those who speak in God's name (2 Sam. 12:7; Acts 4:18). When someone goes through a dramatic change of life, particularly when that change is divinely initiated, that person's old name will not do. A new name is given for a new identity (Gen. 17:5; 17:15; 32:28; Mark 3:16). A name is not merely a label, an arbitrary designation of someone. A name represents a person's true significance and essence. There is power in a name.

In the Eucharist, when the pastor passes the wine and breaks the bread "in the name of Jesus," a sacrament occurs. As Augustine said of baptism, water is water, but when water is next to the Word, set next to the name of Jesus, "there results the Sacrament, as if itself also is a kind of visible word." Or as Luther rephrased Augustine, baptism is "water used according to God's command and connected with God's word."

The sacraments are visible signs of God's providence, God's daily, mundane care of the world. Sacraments move us from daily acts like eating or bathing to consider other daily acts like greeting and parting, working, touching, healing, speaking, and suggest that they have sacramental significance when done "in the name of Jesus." No good human act, no matter how mundane, is exempt from the possibility of being used as a revelation of God's presence when that act is done "in the name of Jesus." The nurse who washes the patient's feet, the teacher who comforts a crying child, the janitor who helps clean the office, the secretary who answers the phone, all may be used for priestly, providential activity if their activity is done "in the name of Jesus."

On New Year's Day—after all of the partying of the past New Year's Eve and the yuletide hoopla of what the world calls Christmas—as we prepare to resume our mundane, worldly activity in January, worship at the Name of Jesus provides the church with an opportunity to gather "in the name of Jesus" and consider the year ahead for us, to pray that God might bless us so that this year might be lived "in his name."

Second Sunday after Christmas

Lutheran	Roman Catholic	Episcopal	Common Lectionary
Isa. 61:10—62:3	Sir. 24:1-2, 8-12	Jer. 31:7-14	Jer. 31:7-14 *or* Sir. 24:1-2, 8-12
Eph. 1:3-6, 15-18	Eph. 1:3-6, 15-18	Eph. 1:3-6, 15-19a	Eph. 1:3-6, 15-18
John 1:1-18	John 1:1-18	Matt. 2:13-15, 19-23	John 1:1-18

FIRST LESSON: JEREMIAH 31:7-14

"I have loved you with an everlasting love" (Jer. 31:3), says the God who restores these pitiful exiles. Once again in Israel's history, God intervenes, preserving Israel, creating as if out of nothing a people where there had been only ruin. Restoration of Israel after exile is visible, tangible, historical, fleshly testimony that "I have continued my faithfulness to you" (Jer. 31:3). Thus today's first lesson suggests that Christmas—the fleshly, incarnational, visible, intrusion of God into our history—is no exclusively New Testament, one-time event. What God was doing in places like Luke 2 and John 1, God had always been busy promising and doing in places like the last joyous chapters of Jeremiah.

Specifically, Jeremiah 31:7-14 is a description of homecoming. "Sing aloud," "raise shouts," "give praise" (31:7) are the fitting responses of people who are at long last back home. Perhaps the preacher might want to ponder contemporary evidence for "exile" as an appropriate metaphor for the condition of many of our people. From what, whom, or where have we become alienated, cut off, dispersed? Under what conditions might we be able to return home? What grand, Christmas announcement might "turn their mourning into joy," might "give them gladness for sorrow" (31:13)?

The Christmas holidays are popular times for people to return to their home church for visits with friends and relatives. There may be a larger than usual number of people in the congregation who, having once wandered away from the church, feel some vague need to return to church during Christmas. We preachers ought not to despise their sense of need, their yuletide return for one more look at the church. Today's text invites us to name their seasonal visit to church as a potential "homecoming."

The problem of homelessness is much on our minds. Here is an appropriate metaphor, not only for failed government economic policy, but also an image for how many of us feel. The interpreter of this text may appropriately ask, How can we be brought back home? Under what conditions can God lead us home? Embodied in Jeremiah's promise of homecoming are assumptions about social relations, convictions about the social configurations required for true homecoming.

Also, combined with today's Gospel (John 1:1-18), the preacher may note how though we could not come home to God, God came home to us, pitched God's tent among us, made our flesh God's habitation. Homecoming can work in a number of directions and this Sunday it may be a false choice as to whether we celebrate because we have come home to God or because God has come home to us.

SECOND LESSON: EPHESIANS 1:3-6; 15-18

There are two major ways to have children, to have a family—birth and adoption. Today's Gospel speaks of a power "to become children of God" (John 1:12) which is birth "not of blood or of the will of the flesh . . . but of God" (John 1:13). In John's "Word" new children have been created for God.

The writer to the Ephesians draws another familial metaphor into service, that of adoption. God has "blessed us in Christ" because "he chose us" (Eph. 1:3-4), "for adoption as his children through Jesus Christ" (Eph. 1:5). The image is surely meant to remind us of our baptism. In baptism, we are adopted into the church, thereby qualified to share in "the riches of his glorious inheritance among the saints" (Eph. 1:18).

The church has long spoken of Christ as the means by which God came to us because we could not come to God, the mode by which God became human so that we humans could become as God. Reaching for intimate, familial metaphors of birth and adoption, the writer to the Ephesians is attempting to speak of an inexpressible mystery—the incarnation. Christ was as close to God as we can be. Everything that God has to give, Christ has to give.

What God was doing in Christ was not only intimate and familial, it was also large and cosmic. It was an event that touched us here, solidly on earth, but that resounded "in the heavenly places" (Eph. 1:3), something ordained "before the foundation of the world" (Eph. 1:4, compare with today's Gospel, esp. John 1:1-3).

Whatever we say about this Sunday, full in to Christmas, deep in the mystery of the incarnation, we must sing it in two-part harmony, we must somehow do justice to the advent of the Christ as a cosmic, heavenly event with utterly earthly consequences.

GOSPEL: JOHN 1:1-18

John's Gospel is the product of some early Christian community that has been blinded by the light of the risen Christ. In their weekly experiences of the Eucharist, in their life together, in their speaking and hearing of Gospel words, they had become convinced that, in Jesus, "the Word became flesh and lived among us, and we have seen his glory, the glory as of a father's only son, full of grace and truth" (John 1:14). It is also a community locked in fierce polemic with friends and relatives who have not seen and experienced the same light ("He came to what was his own, and his own people did not accept him," John 1:11). We need not attempt to continue such polemic against any group of long-forgotten antagonists, unless we wish to address it to ourselves, present preachers and congregations who, having sung of this "light" for close to two thousand years now, show so little of its radiance in our daily lives.

Our reflection on John 1:1-18 would do better to avoid any gloomy polemic today. (Carping sermons on Christmas materialism and over-consumption are not only too late by this Sunday but also of questionable theological significance by this point. Our three exuberant texts are for singing, not scolding.) Through magnificent, deeply beloved evangelical cadences, John wants us to sing of that astounding, continuing incarnational reality, "The light shines in the darkness, and the darkness did not overcome it" (1:5).

The prologue is the whole of John's Gospel in miniature, "the Word was with God, and the Word was God" (1:1). The NEB's rendering "what God was, the Word was" is perhaps more to the point of John's theology here. While John means to keep "the Word" distinct from God, everything that God has, is, and does also lives in the Word. Here is the great scandal of the Christian faith, the stumbling block to many of our neighbors' religions. We Christians really believe that, in this earthly, fleshly Jew from Nazareth named Jesus, we have seen the fullness of the light of God. This prologue hymn is an amazing theological claim that "the Word became flesh and lived among us" (1:14a). The "lived among us" is more literally rendered "pitched his tent among us," perhaps evoking memories of the tabernacle of God in the midst of wandering Israel (see Num. 35:34). While the language here sounds exalted (and is), it is meant to convey a very earthly, extremely mundane event—"the Word became flesh and lived among us."

The Episcopal Lectionary's Gospel for this Sunday is Matthew 2:13-15, 19-23, the account of a refugee family's flight into Egypt. The flight into Egypt is Matthew's more narrative rendering of John 1:10, "the world did not know him" and John 1:11, "his own people did not accept him." These sober facts, clothed in John's polemic against the synagogue ("his own people did not accept him") are even more dramatically illustrated by Herod's slaughter of the innocents (Matt. 2:16-18) which are unjustifiably omitted from the lectionary. Matthew wants us to know that, just over the hill from Luke's "O Little Town of Bethlehem" (Luke 2) lies a less hospitable hill named "The Place of the Skull" (Mark 15:22). Coupled with John 1:10-11, Matthew's story of the flight into Egypt could be a helpful, sobering corrective to our natural inclination to escape the political, eschatological significance of the incarnation by flights, not to Egypt with the holy family, but into yuletide sentimentality and romanticism with Bing Crosby.

PROCLAIMING THE TEXTS

Few congregations go looking for new Christmas carols. Part of the fun of Christmas is that even the most disinterested singer of hymns knows all the verses of every Christmas hymn. We can sing them "by heart." As if to affirm the joy of the familiar and the eternally beloved, the lectionaries (with the exception of the Episcopal) have us read the prologue to John one more time on those years when two Sundays occur in the twelve days between Christmas and Epiphany. Today we shall sing all twelve stanzas of John's hymn one more time before we leave the joyous feast of the incarnation. We are to sing these glorious cadences until we know them "by heart."

Of course, one of the problems with a familiar hymn or biblical pericope is that we know it so well that we cease to know it, really know it. Thus, today's Gospel invites the preacher creatively to listen again to John 1:1-18 in the hope that it may be heard as if for the first time, as if, by hearing it again, this Sunday might be a "homecoming" for us all (Jer. 31:7-14).

Just to sing, "And the Word became flesh and lived among us, and we have seen his glory, the glory as of the father's only son, full of grace and truth" (John 1:14), is in itself a world-changing, revolutionary act. Just to say this is to throw all other rulers, epistemologies, and descriptions of reality into crisis. If it is true, and we are busy believing it to be, that in this "Word" we have seen God (John 1:1), this is also to relativize all other claimants for ultimate allegiance. These verses are commonly called the prologue to John's Gospel, the beginning, the prelude to the symphony. Let us take them, read as they are here at the beginning of a new calendar year, as a fitting prologue to the coming year in Christ.

Yet these opening verses also say much about our end. In this Word, who was "in the beginning" (1:1), everything else has come to an end, an *eschaton*. *Finis* (finish) is theologically related to *telos* (goal). So we Christians tend to use that word "end" in a twofold sense. Our time is the *eschaton*, not only in the political sense that, in the advent of the Word, all other penultimate principalities and powers have come to an end, caput, are done with, have had their day; but also in the light of the Word, we see our true end, the goal, the ultimate point of it all.

John makes much, in his prologue, about the beginning of all things. He begins his Gospel at the beginning, at the very beginning, all the way back in Genesis 1. Right from the start, from ground zero of the whole cosmos, *"en arche,"* in the beginning the Word was what the Creator had in mind, the Word was the mind of the Creator. Yet everything in John's Gospel is meant to be read "backwards" as it were, from Easter and resurrection back through the cross, the cleansing of the temple, turning water to wine, all the way back through Jesus' baptism, racing backward to the very beginning of time, back before there was time, to where there was not even a world—there, there was "the Word with God."

> *Of the Father's love begotten, ere the world began to be,*
> *He is Alpha and Omega, he the source, the ending he*
> *Of the things that are, that have been, and that future*
> *   years shall see,*
> *Evermore and evermore.*
>
> ("Of the Father's Love Begotten,"
> Aurelius Clemens Prudentius,
> trans. John Mason Neale, 1851
> and Henry W. Baker, 1859)

Let us avoid the tragic interpretive mistake of assuming that because John 1:1-18 contains some poetry, some very beautiful poetry with some strange images, that it is concerned alone with things ethereal and heavenly. John wisely intersperses talk of John the Baptist, the great "witness to testify to the light" (1:7), to link the historical and the temporal with the eternal and the heavenly. Real, controversial, historical figures are enlisted to testify to the reality of the Christ. (See the discussion of John's John the Baptist on the Third Sunday in Advent.) John is convinced that it is from within the earthly, the bodily, the daily, the fleshly, the corporeal that divine light shines. "And the Word became flesh and lived among us, . . ." (1:14). Perhaps this invites homiletical reflection on the ways in which, since the incarnation, we experience the eternal Word revealed in our temporal affairs.

Isn't it odd that John's Gospel should have developed a reputation for spiritualized, highly exalted Christology, when throughout, John is intent to show how in the everyday affairs of people—like weddings, dinners, evening visits, hellos and good-byes—we see the glory of God.

As Alpha and Omega, the Word is all creation as it is meant to be, the beginning of all things and therefore the end as well. Cosmic normality, nothing begins without the Word (1:1-3). Linking Genesis 1:1—2:4a with the incarnation, John reminds us how "the Word" brought all things into being. In a similar way, by the act of speaking and hearing the words of this Gospel, a new world is being evoked. *Ex nihilo*, a new people is being formed. Many of those who ought to have heard the Word "did not accept him" (1:11). "But to all who received him, who believed in his name, he gave power to become children of God" (1:12). In the church, in the gathering of those who hear and believe "the Word," a new world is happening, a new baptismally derived family (see Eph. 1:3-5) is being formed. The church is a new act of divine creation through the Word.

In the Word, a claim is also being made about the end. Here, at the beginning of a New Year and at the end of the old, as the world around the church prepares merely to flip over a new page on the calendar without much meaning attached to it, the church pauses to ponder the most mysterious and majestic of our affirmations of faith: The Word made flesh among us, the One who stood at the beginning, creating a new people out of nothing, is also the One who meets us at the end. Alpha and Omega, Christmas, the incarnation, is far too cosmic, too large to be encapsulated in the world's limited definitions. Alpha and Omega, January 1 and December 31, we peer into the manger at Bethlehem (Luke 2) and see where we have come from and where, by the "grace and truth" of God (John 1:14), we are going. This is the Sunday that says, in sublime, poetic utterance, the significance of our birth and death, the whole world's beginning and end, is grace, upon grace, upon grace.